Chap

Stay-At-Hom

`CW00616254`

Illustrations by Alasdair Gray, David Schofield, Hazel Terry and Kara Wilson.

ISBN 0 906772 93 1   ISSN 0308-2695   © *Chapman* 2000

CHAPMAN

4 Broughton Place, Edinburgh EH1 3RX, Scotland
E-mail: editor@chapman-pub.co.uk
Website: www.chapman-pub.co.uk
Tel 0131–557 2207 Fax 0131–556 9565

Editor: Joy Hendry   **Assistant Editor: Gerry Stewart**

Volunteers: Valerie Brotherton, Hannah Eckberg, Serena Field.

Submissions:
Chapman welcomes submissions of poetry, fiction and articles provided they are accompanied by a stamped addressed envelope or International Reply Coupons

Subscriptions:

	Personal		Institutional	
	1 year	2 years	1 year	2 years
UK	£16	£30	£20	£38
Overseas	£21/$35	£39/$65	£25/$43	£47$75

THE SCOTTISH ARTS COUNCIL

Printed by Inglis Allen, Middlefield Road, Falkirk FK2 9AG

Edinburgh Book Festival Post Office Lecture
Scotland and the World

Edwin Morgan

One of the lords of the internet in America, Nicholas Negroponte, has been quoted recently as saying: "Ten to twenty years from now, kids won't care much about countries". The internet is almost science fiction. If you ask what it is, or where it is, you will get an answer, but the answer may not be satisfying or even very clear. But of course it is not science fiction; it is very real, and millions join it every month. It is truly a world-wide web, and because it is interactive anyone in one country can tap or click into anyone from another country without perhaps, and I emphasise perhaps, knowing or caring much about geographical or cultural identity. One can wander into the world-wide web rather as a poet would wander into a wood in some medieval romance, in search of nothing more specific than adventures, surprises, novelties, the unknown and the strange. It is a perfect escapist toy as well as a sophisticated tool for extracting information. But is Negroponte right? Does it blank out countries? A few weeks ago I had a phone call from California, from the Jay Leno *Tonight Show,* saying that they had come across my name on the internet as a Scottish poet, and thought they might like to have me on their show. Did I have a video of myself, talking about my life and reading a few poems, which I could send? I didn't, but knowing that Americans don't like people to be negative I said I would get one made. So I made a ten-minute video and sent it off. I am still, as they say, waiting by the telephone. But the interesting thing is that they got, from the internet, something specifically Scottish, and acted on it. They wanted to hear a voice from a country that to them was fairly exotic, and without the internet they might never have even thought about it. As long as this kind of incident can happen, it seems to me that Negroponte's prediction that globalisation will simply melt all national boundaries and identities is, as the lawyers say, unsafe.

How much of this is totally new, and what continuities are there? Scotland, being the remoter part of an offshore island of a large continent, has always had to think about its place in the scheme of things, and, apart from one or two inward-gazing periods it has taken up the challenge with vigour. People speak about "visiting a site" on the internet, and this form of words shows how persistent the idea is of physically going to other places which you either know about and want to investigate or want to know more because you know so little, or – a third possibility – places of legendary import which may or may not exist, Shangri-la, Xanadu, even Timbuktu, but which are certainly different from high street or the village square. From this point of view the Scots have always been great travellers, wanderers, explorers, sometimes from economic necessity, sometimes in the spirit of adventure, but always keeping Scotland usefully exposed to the rest of the

Photograph by Kevin Low

world. What our literature has gained or lost from the footloose army is something I shall be looking at. Meantime, we shouldn't forget the alternative exploratory possibility, not through physical action but through the translation of foreign texts. Scotland has plunged enthusiastically into translation, especially in the medieval and Renaissance periods and the 20th century. Interest in other languages and therefore other countries and cultures probably emerged from the mixed and volatile language situation in early Scotland itself. Gaelic, Welsh, Norse, Anglo-Saxon, Latin and Pictish were all spoken, and all except Pictish also written. Translators and interpreters must have been in great demand. We know that when St Columba travelled from Iona to talk to and hopefully convert the pagan King Brude of the Picts, he had an interpreter with him, and this situation must have been repeated often from the 5th to the 11th centuries, when the northern form of Anglo-Saxon began to be dominant. A certain language interest, a certain language orientation, has remained with Scottish writers ever since.

Monuments of Scottish translating activity are not wanting. Gavin Douglas's version of Virgil's *Aeneid*, finished in 1513, was its earliest translation into any branch of English. Douglas called his language 'Scottis', not 'Inglis' or 'Suddroun', to indicate his sense of difference, and in line with the vernacular revivals all over Europe. He was showing his solidarity with Europe, but was also anxious to prove that his own almost marginally European Scottish language could go a good part of the way in meeting the Latin challenge of Virgil. As a pragmatic translator, he knows that Scots and English are sister tongues, and he is not scared to use an English word where necessary, as he tells us in his Prologue to Book I:

> And yet forsooth I set my busy pain
> As that I couth, to make it braid and plain,
> Kepand na Sudroun bot our own langage,
> And speakis as I lernit when I was page.
> Nor yet sa clean all Sudroun I refuse
> Bot some word I pronounce as nychbour dois.
> Like as in Latin bene Greek termis some . . .

A less known but remarkable 16th century translation is John Stewart's version of Ariosto's *Orlando Furioso,* called *Roland Furious.* Although English was beginning to be much more used in Scotland, Stewart pulls out all the stops to be Scottish, as in the passage describing the onset of Orlando's madness:

> He raifs, he rugs, he bruisis, breaks and ryfs
> With hands, with feit, with nails and teith alway;
> He byts, he stricks, he tumbls, he turns, he stryfs,
> He glaiks, he gaips, he girns, he glours, he dryfs
> Throw moss and montane, forrest, firth and plaine,
> The birds, the beists, the boyes, the men and wyfs,
> With bruit moir hiddeus from his troublit braine
> Than force of fluidis hurlland in great raine.
> Foull glar and dust his face all filthie meed,
> Quhairin no former beutie did remaine
> And both his eis for wraith was boudin reed,

Quhilks up and doune ay turnit in his heed
With fearce regard upcasting all the quhyt.

Among translations into English, in the 17th century, the most notable is clearly Thomas Urquhart's version of Rabelais, which is more Rabelaisian than the original. This was a labour of love, and a major undertaking, and its exuberance has kept it in print even today when more accurate translations are available. Scottish translating activity had a strong revival in the 20th century, when Hugh MacDiarmid, Robert Garioch, Sydney Goodsir Smith, Alastair Mackie, Robin Fulton and many others reopened contacts with the rest of the world which had been allowed to lapse. Tentacles were sent out to German, Russian, Italian, French, Spanish, Greek, Norwegian, Swedish, Polish, Hungarian: quite an impressive lassoing of international writers. And by now there is a pleasing reciprocity: there are translations of modern Scottish poets into French, German, Italian, Polish, Hungarian and other languages. The isolation of (say) the 19th century has been decisively broken.

But what about the other, physical sort of contact mentioned earlier? Thousands of Scots from the 14th century onwards made their way to northern Europe, to Denmark and Sweden and Poland and especially Russia. They went as workmen, as traders, as mercenaries, or simply as adventurers. Many of them settled, and their names can still be seen in disguised form today. The soldiers and sailors of fortune often rose to high rank. James Murray and Samuel Greig practically established the Polish and Russian navies. A century before their time, General Patrick Gordon when he lay dying had the supreme honour of having his eyelids closed by Peter the Great himself. In the cultural sphere, the architect Charles Cameron put up fine buildings for Catherine the Great and other patrons; and the early Scottish photographer William Carrick made a remarkable record of everyday Russian life. And just to mention the two-way process: it's not widely known that Adam Smith had Russian students in his political economy classes at Glasgow University (an interesting speculation there, perhaps), and a distinguished Russian visitor to Walter Scott, Vladimir Davydov, made him the first person in Britain to read a translation of the medieval epic *The Lay of Igor's Raid*.

Moving west instead of east, it is possible, even probable, that Henry Sinclair, Earl of Orkney, discovered America in 1398, a century before Columbus, sailing round Newfoundland and landing on Nova Scotia. If we are not entirely certain about his voyages, we have no doubt about one intrepid traveller in the 17th century. William Lithgow, known as Lugless Will because his ears were cut off by the brothers of a girl he was courting, was born in Lanark, and it is thought that his shame and embarrassment in Lanarkshire, not the most tolerant of counties, started him off on his extraordinary series of travels, later recorded by himself in his book, *The Rare Adventures and Painful Peregrinations of William Lithgow* (1632). This is one of the really great travel books, much admired by Graham Greene, but still not nearly as well known as it ought to be. Lithgow was a born observer, curious about everything, both places and people, and able to write vividly and racily and often with the animated and artful alliterations of the time. He was physically tough, journeying on foot wherever he could, overcoming disease and pirates and footpads and every kind of menace and chicanery. He visited Italy, Greece, Turkey, Syria, Palestine, Egypt, Hungary, Poland, Germany, Ireland, Spain and Morocco. He crossed the Sahara Desert. He thought Cairo the finest city in the world, and after Cairo, Constantinople. It's particularly interesting that he was attracted by two non-European, Muslim cities. This was Scotland and the world, not Scotland and Europe. He himself has a comment on this, on what he calls "the science of the world":

> This is it above all things that preferreth men to honours and the charges that make great houses and republics to flourish, and render the actions and words of them who possess it agreeable both to great and small. This science is only acquired by conversation and haunting the company of the most experimented; by divers discourses, reports, by writs, or by a lively voice, in communicating with strangers; and in the judicious consideration of the living with one another; and above all and principally by travellers and voyagers in divers regions and remote places, whose experience confirmeth the true science thereof and can best draw the anatomy of human condition.

Since he liked Egypt so much, it's worth mentioning two of his observations. As he is wandering through Cairo, he notices a certain sexual confusion:

> They also use here, as commonly they do in Turkey, the women to piss standing, and the men to cower low on their knees doing the like. They wear here linen breeches and leather boots, and if it were not for their covered faces and longer gowns we would hardly know the one from the other.

Later he climbed the Great Pyramid, and in his meticulous way he gives measurements of what he found. He tries but cannot understand how the huge blocks were set in place, but his most interesting observation concerns the summit:

> Truly, the more I beheld this strange work, the more I was stricken in admiration: for before we ascended or came near to this pyramid the top of it seemed as sharp as a diamond, but when we were mounted thereon we found it so large that in my opinion it would have contained a hundred men.

Lithgow did not know that the worst of his travels was to be his last. He never hid his Protestant beliefs, and when he went to Malaga in Spain he was arrested as a spy and handed over to the Inquisition. He was tortured, over long periods, on the rack, but of course had nothing to confess, and he was about to be burnt at the stake when the English consul accidentally heard about his case and secured his release. He got back home, but was crippled for life. He was only able to write his book because his right arm was relatively unharmed. The story of this Scot, once read, surely deserves the adjective unforgettable.

The argument of stay-at-home versus dusty-foot can never be resolved. What is right for one could be wrong for another. Emily Brontë did not have to stir from Haworth in order to write *Wuthering Heights*, which is intensely local, down to its careful transcriptions of West Yorkshire dialect, and yet is absolutely universal in its treatment of themes of love and revenge and family continuities. It would be bad if we let enthusiasm for world-mindedness downgrade Hopkins's *haecceitas*, the thisness of here and now and nowhere else, the pleasure we received from something truthful and restricted. Whatever else Alasdair Gray's *Lanark* and Irvine Welsh's *Trainspotting* have to reveal about life and the universe, these are books about Glasgow and Edinburgh respectively, and tell truths concerning the two places which have not been told before and which are worth telling. If a writer is a born traveller, like Robert Louis Stevenson, he will write about his various jaunts and voyages – *An Inland Journey, Travels with a Donkey in the Cévennes, The Silverado Squatters, In the South Seas*. Splendid tales? Well, sort of. But they lack the distinction of his four masterly novels. Everyone feels a slight disappointment with Stevenson, a lack of solidity, a sense of travelling rather than arriving. This may well be due to a restlessness related to his illness, and therefore we attach no blame. But it does help us to think about the many questions that are raised by the residence versus non-residence argument. These questions relate both to the kind of writing and to the quality of writing in the person concerned. They concern the writer's fame or reputation. They may lead to debates about definition which can seem paltry but which do continue to exercise inquiring minds. Joseph Conrad left his native Poland and became a celebrated novelist in English, a language he never totally mastered. The occasional oddities of his style even add a distinctive flavour which most people rather like. Yet there are books and articles in Poland which discuss him as a Polish novelist, a novelist-in-exile whose work gives clear indications of his Slavonic nature and upbringing. Conrad's reputation as an English novelist seems secure, but it may be that we ought, in discussing him, to pay more attention to his origins and (if there is such a thing) national psychology.

One Scottish writer who admired Conrad and was admired by him in return is Cunninghame Graham, whom I'd like to have a look at. Graham (1852-1936) has had a rocky and uncertain kind of fame. Greatly respected by distinguished contemporaries, though never a hugely popular writer, he has been steadily neglected since his death, with periodic attempts at revival by enthusiasts. One of the two reasons for this is the feeling that someone so physically active and adventurous could hardly be a serious writer. He was an expert horseman, cattle-drover, lassoer, fencer and shooter; he made dangerous expeditions into South America and North Africa; he was beaten up by the police during a demonstration in Trafalgar Square; he made fiery speeches as a left-Liberal MP in the House of Commons and later became President of the National Party of Scotland which eventually evolved into the SNP. His self-dramatisation and love of dressing up did not help: he enjoyed strutting through London in a large Spanish hat and elaborate riding-boots, so that the London *Times* called him a "cowboy dandy". Well, perhaps he was a cowboy dandy. He was certainly an individualist, an eccentric, an aristocrat who championed the cause of the working class at every point. But was he a good writer, and was he a good Scottish writer?

His work falls into two parts. He wrote a series of biographies of the Spanish *conquistadores* in South America. These books are not among his most successful, being largely based on earlier writers and being uncomfortably ambiguous in tone. He did not hide or excuse the brutalities and cruelties of the conquerors of Mexico and Peru, but as a man of action himself also could not hide his admiration for the qualities of toughness, persistence and single-mindedness that the Spaniards evinced. From a Scottish viewpoint, perhaps the most notable feature of these books is their being constantly peppered with Scottish words, phrases and references, as if he was determined not to let readers forget that he was not an English writer. (This is probably in line with the fact that he always came back home from his various expeditions; he never thought of himself as an exile.) You find phrases like "The Catalans are the Scotch of Spain", "the snell wind of the Pampas", "he drees his weird", "the national (Venezuelan) dance is as quick as a Scotch reel and just as violent", a Brazilian friar "preached a sermon of the kind known to Scotch theologians as Erastian, a mere cold morality, very unsatisfying to the soul". Although we may feel inclined to write off these books, they have many passages of insight and observation that stick in the mind. Here is something seen in Buenos Aires. A group of elderly men in their 70s and 80s are gathered together at a window that looks onto the street, reminiscing about past exploits while they drink maté and watch the evening darken into night.

> The negro girl, or Paraguayan Indian, in their white dresses, their bare feet making a slapping on the floor like indiarubber, went and came, serving maté, silently waiting till the guest had sucked the boiling liquid through the silver tube. Outside, amongst the orange trees in the patio, the fireflies flitted to and fro, like stars that had gone adrift from heaven, amongst the dark metallic leaves. Sometimes a visitor would ride up to the grated window, rein up his horse and greet the company. Without dismounting, he would take a maté passed to him though the bars, sit listening silently, perhaps for a full hour, with a leg resting on his horse's neck and his great silver spur hung loosely from the heel. Then when the watchman's voice resounded through the silent street, informing the good citizens that in the name of the most Holy Virgin it was twelve o'clock, and a serene night, the rider, shifting back into his seat, would salute the company and vanish noiselessly along the sandy street.

In one sense this is a Scottish writer using a surface exoticism – the fireflies, the orange trees, the maté being sucked through a silver tube – but Graham makes it more than that by bringing in the mysterious figure of the rider, about whom nothing is known, who rides in and rides out, but who is courteous and respectful to the old men telling their stories. Graham is fond of introducing such solitary figures, and through them to be saying something about place and identity, about wandering and searching. In another story ('Animula Vagula'), set in Colombia, the narrator is an orchid-hunter who has to deal with the body of a young man brought to him by Native Americans. The body has no identification papers; the man has blue eyes and is probably British or American; but nothing is known about him

– had he any family, where did he come from, where was he going to? There is some pathos, but more realism. This is something that happens. Those who travel the jungles of the world will come across many such cases. The man was, as the Spanish say, "un infeliz", an unhappy one, an unfortunate one, and yet, as the narrator says, "perhaps fortunate in that interior world to which so many eyes are closed". At the end of the story the orchid-hunter himself melts back into the jungle, and there is a strong suggestion that he too may be 'un infeliz'. The theme of uprootedness is a very Scottish one, and Graham clearly felt himself to be involved in these thoughts and feelings.

The second reason for Graham's insecure reputation is the uncategorisability of his best writing, which occurs in many books of, let us call them, short stories which he brought out between 1900 and 1936. Some of these short pieces are fictional, some are reminiscence, some are documentary, and many are an amalgam of the three approaches that leaves the reader either puzzled and disoriented or delighted at Graham's tantalisingly fresh approach. Also, in any one book the settings are randomised, so that you move from South America to North Africa to Scotland to England to the high seas. Critics used to despair at all this irrationality, but it seems to me that with a certain openness we have nowadays it is possible to see Graham as a non-conformist ahead of his time. Here, for example, are three consecutive stories from the collection *A Hatchment* (1913). 'A Moral Victory' is a humorous story a little reminiscent of John Galt, set in Yorkshire but with Scottish connections, and it begins like this:

My Aunt Alexia, whom I remember vividly, though she died more than forty years ago, was a type of the Yorkshire gentlewoman now long extinct. Short, and dark-haired, with eyes that seemed to be on the point of starting from her head, she had a strong and wiry moustache, and when by chance she did not pull it out, a growth of beard upon her chin, which used to make me shudder when as a boy she kissed me and they grated on the skin. I do not think this outward, visible sign of masculine interior forces gave her much trouble or annoyance, for she would say with pride, "My cousins the Fitzgibbons all have beards, both women and men alike." Family pride was a strong point with my good aunt.

From that entertaining tale you move to 'Bismillah' (In the Name of God), set in North Africa in a hot, peaceful landscape where a boy is looking after a herd of goats. One white kid attaches itself to the boy. It is not a pet, but for some reason follows him about, and he regards it almost as if it were a dog. Towards the end of the day the flock is brought back to the village. One of the village elders approaches the boy, takes the little white kid, and after saying "In the name of God" cuts its throat with a sharp knife. Its time had come. The goatherd, with Arab stoicism, expresses no protest or grief. Graham accepts that this is what happens. No sentimentality would be correct. But he adds, at the close of the tale:

Mystery of mysteries! Still the same air of peace hung over everything, and as the flock passed to its pen the call to prayer was wafted up to heaven from the village mosque, fitful and quavering.

The last phrase, "fitful and quavering", suggests that perhaps all is not so well after all; the sound is very like the voice of a goat.

That story is followed by what is virtually a prose poem, 'Mist in Menteith'. The Lake of Menteith was Graham's home territory, and he had strong feelings about that part of Scotland. He describes the frequent mists and their immediate, often mysterious effects on the landscape as they roll about, thicken, disperse, re-form. They suggest change, disguise, loss of identity. Historically, they sheltered marauders from the north. Today, they create strange sound-effects. "Over the whole earth hangs, as it were, a sounding-board, intensifying everything, making the senses more acute, and carrying voices from a distance, focused to the ear." The whole piece is a sort of off-beat homage to his native place.

Graham was very Scottish, a convinced Nationalist who did something about it by becoming a political activist. This was why Hugh MacDiarmid admired him so much, but others were alienated by what they thought was his antics on horseback all over South America. What on earth was he doing there? To Graham, it wasn't antics. He was following in the footsteps of the *conquistadores* who in his opinion had brought about one of the most awesome historical changes. Unlike the conquest of North America, where the Native Americans had a nomadic culture but no settled civilisation, the Spanish conquest attacked a sophisticated, literate, complex group of civilisations, some of whose cities were greater than anything in Spain at that time. And these civilizations were obliterated, they did not recover. The fact that the native cultures had their own cruelties and brutalities, as the Spaniards had, means that you cannot take a simple moralistic view, but the total destruction means we shall never know how Inca or Aztec society might have developed: an entire avenue of history has been closed. Graham's interest in these things shows him as a citizen of the world, and helps to keep him, in my opinion, one Scottish writer we shouldn't be ignorant of.

Graham is at least vaguely known to the general public, but in the diaspora or semi-diaspora of Scots there are some writers who seem to have slipped off the national memory fairly completely. I'd like to talk about one of these, in the hope of bringing her back into the fold. The poet Helen Adam (1909-1993) belonged to the same generation as Norman MacCaig and Sorley MacLean, but unlike them she lived a large part of her life in another country, with the most remarkable result. Born in Glasgow, where her father was a Presbyterian minister, she was brought up in the north-east of Scotland, and after a spell at Edinburgh University she did journalistic work in Edinburgh and London. She was precocious as a writer, and had two volumes of poetry published when in her early teens. The poems were dreamlike, in English, and in a faded Victorian style, and no one looking at these books, or at *Shadow of the Moon* (1929) would have prophesied she would become an interesting and original poet. But in 1939 she went with her mother and sister to America, and her second life began.

She was living at first in New York, but felt an inevitable tug to the west, and made San Francisco her home. This was in the early 1950s, when the Beat movement and the San Francisco Renaissance were being hatched, and she effortlessly linked herself into the new movements, becoming friendly with Allen Ginsberg and Robert Duncan, and soon being renowned as a spellbinding performer of her own poems, which were now largely in Scots and closely related to the old Scottish ballad tradition. She published many books, some beautifully produced by the small American avant-garde presses, many illustrated with line drawings or collages. The most remarkable collages are her own, often based on Victorian black-and-white engravings but sometimes with a brilliant splash of blue for butterflies or flowers: dark forests, wild seascapes, standing stones, a woman with a cat's head, cats playing with a woman's head, despairing figures marooned in savage gulfs of rock and water – clearly influenced by surrealist art but evoking the atmosphere of her own violent and often supernatural poems.

Her master subject was love in all its manifestations, but especially those that were not likely to lead to a happily lasting outcome. Jilting, two-timing, jealousy, adultery, idealised search, unrequited passion, over-requited passion, murderous revenge – these are her field of operations, and however bizarre the circumstances she at times would place her characters in, a deep psychological insight was at work. In 'I Love my Love', a man marries a woman with long bright hair, and after a honeymoon period finds that her love is overpowering, stifling, binding, deadly as a web he must break out from; he comes desperate and kills her, but her hair takes a grim revenge by escaping from the grave and smothering him: "There was no sound but the joyful hiss of the sweet insatiable hair".

Men are more often the victims than women in these poems, and the women are often presented as virtual or real sorceresses. In the long poem 'The Queen o' Crow Castle', the fearsome crow-attended Queen, whose real lover is the Deil, has killed off seven husbands, and the corbies look forward to the eighth:

> Haw, craw, craw haw, kra caw crackarus! . . .
> Ain, twa, three, four, five, six, seven. Craw!
> Swakked doun, bogle bit, caught up skirling, banes brackled,
> Skulls crunched, clapped clawed, dunted.
> Dust and ashes, dead gone, dead gone.
> Kra, craw, clap, slap, eight will be you.

But the circumstances do not need to be supernatural. In one of her strongest poems, 'Miss Laura', a girl in the US South has a passionate affair with a black groom, later denounces him to the white supremacists, and after the inevitable lynching is haunted to madness by what she has done: she cannot stop talking:

> Love me, Honey, where Savannah flows,
> Love me naked. Throw away my clothes.
>
> My body's open, and I want you in.
> Black, black, black, black is the colour
> Of my true lover's skin.

She again used English in a striking poem called 'Rime of a Prince of Sodom', where the destruction of the Biblical city is described not as an awful warning but with sympathy and sorrow, by the men of Sodom themselves, who regret the loss of "Love's game long hidden,/ Or by fools forbidden".

Not bad for a daughter of the manse! there are in fact a number of poems on gay or lesbian themes. The most powerful one is in Scots, 'The Fair Flowery Lea', where the handsome hero, Dalgarth, makes the mistake of having an affair with the young wife of the Clerk o' Kintire, who happens to be a wizard. The Clerk sends a fiery demon to kill him, but the demon is transfixed by the beauty of Dalgarth and instead of killing him wants to make love to him. Dalgarth lives on, inseparable from his gay demon. Anyone watching would see "frae the forest the twa lovers steal,/ Dalgarth in his beauty wi' Hell at his heel".

Sadness replaces terror in one of the English poems, where a girl is the victim. The speaker has been jilted by a sailor in San Francisco and has become a streetwalker, endlessly promiscuous, always seeking sailors:

> And when the fog rolls through San Francisco,
> And shrouds the streets of that famous town,
> Across the darkness he throws me roses.
> My bed is thorny when I lie down.
> I sleep with strangers. I sleep with strangers.
> My bed is thorny when I lie down.

In her more realistic poems, San Francisco is never far way, with references to junkies and muggers, Haight-Ashbury's beatniks and hipsters and hustlers, Nob Hill's millionaires, and all the strident activities of a seatown. But surface realism is not quite her mode, and when she falls back on imagination, or indeed on phantasmagoria, her pen takes off and quivers and barks with delight. (I think her fondness for the dog-headed god Anubis got into that last sentence.)

Her number one phantasmagoria is the extraordinary ballad opera, *San Francisco's Burning* (1963), performed in San Francisco and New York, with Adam playing one of the main parts. The title refers to the three days of fires which followed the disastrous San Francisco earthquake of 1906, and the play is set in the days just before the earthquake, developing a sense of foreboding which is partly nightmarish and partly black comedy. With its jazzy rhythms and rhymes, the play is sometimes reminiscent of Bertolt Brecht, but there are all sorts of underpinnings from Adam's reading – Blake and Swedenborg, Frazer's *Golden Bough*, the Tarot cards, Ancient Egyptian religion – and Scotland is not forgotten, as there is a 'Scotch Sailor' who wears a tattered red kilt and speaks in Scots. This last detail suggests, rightly, that it is very much a piece to be seen and heard in performance rather than silently read on the page. In its own unconventional way, the play is a tribute to the city she has adopted and come to love. Her characters are carefully described: Mrs Mackie Rhodus, a dragon of a dowager; Spangler Jack, the King of the Gamblers; the Well Kept Man, a flash gigolo; Mother Bronson's Babies, pretty waterfront girls;

Mrs Valentine, young, vivid, beautiful, ruthless; Handsome Barty White, a wealthy Nob Hill bachelor; the Hanged Man, Ruler of the Underworld; and the Worm Queen, Queen of the world of the dead (Adam's own part).

As the characters' names suggest, the play takes place in two worlds. The Scotch Sailor sings, after he has been killed and is longing for life and love again:

> Twa worlds o' life and death,
> Sae near, sae far apart.
> In between the twa worlds
> The crying o' the heart.

On the more realistic level, the dangerous Mrs Valentine, who has poisoned two husbands and is looking for another, rejoices that she has found a real man when Spangler Jack slaps her face:

> Black angel frowning,
> My sense drowning.
> Oh at last, a ruthless blow.
> Come closer stranger.
> Give me danger.
> Love me low, dear, love me low.
> Don't love me kindly,
> Love roughly, blindly,
> Till the hour when the black cocks crow.
> Let danger take me.
> Let terror shake me.
> Love me low, dear, love me low.

And if you want even greater realism, the sailors who flock to the Hanged Man's House, the worldly playstation of his underworldly machinations, are free with it:

> In the Hanged Man's House, no wrong or right.
> We thrust our fears away,
> With a faggot's love at the dead of night,
> And a tart's at the break of day.
> What's amiss with a faggot's kiss
> When the night's too thick for shame?
> If love's the spark that defies the dark
> In the dark who dares to blame?

Helen Adam is possibly unique in the sense that she would never have made anything of her poetry, even though she wrote a lot of it, had she remained in her native place. She was a latent poet who needed the jolt of an entirely different environment to bring to the surface what was subterraneanly there. Later in life she took out American citizenship, and in American bibliographies she is called an American poet. But that won't do. She was unmistakably a Scottish poet who learned a new boldness and vivacity in California, but who never lost touch with the Scottish oral tradition she grew up with. There is a charming photograph of her at a poetry reading by the young Allen Ginsberg in 1955 – he is wearing a collar and tie and has still to publish *Howl*. She is wearing something black and high-necked and looks quite Presbyterian; her eyes are closed and she is a rapt listener, in the front row. Who would have guessed what tigers were waiting to be

14

unleashed by this demure figure? And what can we learn, if anything, from the story of her life? She was too much of her own woman to be a paradigm. But at least we can say that she moved from Scotland to the world, and made something of it. It would be good for Scotland if we at last claimed her, and that is particularly true today, when there is such a marked sense of wanting to gather up all our forces and makes something of what politicians and referendum have delivered. Even the semi-independence we have, ambiguous though it is, must not be allowed to excuse inaction or apathy. And particularly it must not be allowed to encourage navel-gazing. It was an inspired choice to ask Sheena Wellington to sing Burns's 'For a' that and a' that' at the opening of the new Parliament. No poem of Burns states more clearly the simultaneous urge towards social reform at home and solidarity with and interest in the people of other countries. Burns, supreme local poet though he was, kept a sharp eye open on overseas events, supporting and writing about both French and American Revolutions. There is something gratifying about the fact that his feelings about the brotherhood of man, so candidly (some have said, so naively) expressed have in a sense been reciprocated through his worldwide fame. This is remarkable, and it has surpassed that of the writers who were once his rivals, Walter Scott and James Macpherson. There is a poem by Petőfi, sometimes called the Burns of Hungary, their national bard, who died in his 20s in 1849, fighting for independence from the Russians. The poem is called 'Homer and Ossian', which represents perhaps the peak of the Ossianic mania that swept across Europe. Homer and Ossian are equals, one showing the colour and clarity of Greece, and the other the starkness and gloom of the Celtic northern world; and both are needed. Even in eastern Europe the Ossianic panorama and atmosphere are familiar and are well-described:

> In the land of endless North Sea mists
> with storms massed over savage rocks
> he roars his song in the chaos of the night-time.
> And the moon comes up
> as blood-red as
> the sun that goes down
> and throws its stark light over a wilderness
> haunted by roving clusters
> of spirits, dead warriors mourning
> their last battle.

The excitement and relevance of such lines in the war-torn Europe of the 1840s kept Ossian's name to the fore, but the influence of Burns was more deeply and widely felt, long after such battles were over. The high fantasy of Macpherson could not compete in the end with the down-to-earth realism and pathos of Burns.

In our own century, Hugh MacDiarmid, who lambasted the Burns Cult, would nevertheless agree with Burns that national and international should not be seen as opposing forces but as two sides of the same coin. MacDiarmid's praises of Scotland are many and varied and well-known, and apart from brief foreign trips he stayed in Scotland all his life, but he tried again and again to remind people that his country was only a small part of a greater whole, and that changes which were taking place in human consciousness and were felt in Scotland were world changes. We must look at them, and understand them if we can. There is a passage in his long poem *In Memoriam James Joyce* which deals with just this point:

> Responsibility for the present state of the world
> And for its development for better or worse
> Lies with every single individual;
> Freedom is only really possible
> In proportion as all are free . . .
> World-history and world-philosophy
> Are only now beginning to dawn . . .
> Apart from a handful of scientists and poets
> Hardly anybody is aware of it yet.
> (A society of people without a voice for the consciousness
> That is slowly growing within them)
> Nevertheless everywhere among the great masses of mankind
> With every hour it is growing and emerging.
> Like a mango tree under a cloth,
> Stirring the dull cloth,
> Sending out tentacles.
> – It's not something that can be stopped
> By sticking it away in a zinc-lined box
> Like a tube of radium,
> As most people hope,
> Calling all who approve of it mad.

I love that mango tree stirring under its cloth. The mango is not a Scottish fruit. its exotic provenance, and the slight mystery of what it is doing beneath a cloth, bring MacDiarmid's practice in line with his theory. Great shifts of consciousness, developments in human thought, can take place anywhere in the world, and not necessarily among the so-called advanced nations. Once these developments start, they may seem sinister (like the unseen tentacles of the mango moving under its cloth) or dangerous (like the tube of radium which people want to put away in a zinc-lined box), but to MacDiarmid, on the contrary, they must be encouraged and nurtured and fed into the ethos of every country that wants to be a bold brainy breathing part of the literally and metaphorically turning globe.

Scotland still has hang-ups, shoulder-chips, timorousnesses, but it has a huge chance now of doing away with these things and entering the community of nations. Its writers are well poised to help make this a reality, many of them strongly acknowledged outside Scotland, yet attaining this without diluting or abandoning their origins. This is something which has not happened for a long time, and gives rise to a certain optimism. We do not want a global porridge, a happy-clappy postmodern pluralism; we want serious writers able to be faithful to something in their country which feeds or fascinates them and at the same time to jangle the universal nerve, to pick the mango. Are we a nation? Almost, almost. Another little push and we shall be there. I like to think that the world is ready to welcome it.

This lecture is also available in PN Review.

Gregor Addison

Indalsälven

Indalsälven fights to reach the coast,
twisting its back into crumbling banks.
And one must twist with it
to follow each meaningful stretch.
Each turn into new paths requires its own contortions –
as the great river seeks its definition
against the landscape.
Our talk is of people and their homeland,
those un-named inhabitants
of Sweden's southern coast, Denmark's northern rim,
long ago torn apart by the unifying notion
of borders and nations. That era
which turned oceans into walls.
This is the shape of Sweden less eight meters,
chopped from the record in the last survey;
this is the land where the bark of the birch is chrome
and the light is not let go.

Your uncle Kurt

It was when Russia was Russia
he took to the road.
Finally crossing by the Trans-Siberian railway
into China. He packed seventy years
into a summer suit,
learned wisdom into a soft felt hat.
I heard of him in Stockholm
where he came to earth at last. Perhaps,
his shoes still bide in Leningrad –
and their laces undone –
since the statue of its author was broken up
in the Tourist Revolution.
He filled the pockets of retirement
with the ancient world.
And who knows that there is not still
some of the sand of Egypt
between his toes?

Gikasjön

At 5am the mist rises to 5°
and falls back into the scratched slate of Gikasjön.
Now the white cloud
comes in over Gemon and the half-dark.
The slopes return to the high hills
losing their definition to regain their form.
This road winds south to Vilhelmina,
to the world that awaits.
I feel within to the calm, take it with me,
even as we cross the Kultsjön bridge –
the village side beyond us.

The sky is photographic silver and the lake
a daguerreotype of changing black and grey.
It seems one moment negative
as though we've breached the outer walls,
found our final border,
slipped the comforting clinch of life.
The lake waters brindle and shard,
pockets of calm glinting in the sun, each face
a new aspect. You are cut within me Norrland,
a compass when hopes are few, a map
on which to chart this freedom.

A map of the old world

Ben Lomond on one knee, Atlas
failing to make the lift
but the world intact. The crags in rain,
salt serrate of slate,
egg shell moon crushed into dust.
This crib-becoming prison.
Our compass was the distance of a push-bike's spokes,
the rim compacted grass,
and Saturdays we climbed Carman
each home-coming Columbus.
Our maps were games in fire and bogs,
the shopping centre a slalom course
for trolley cars, and the Bowl O'Meal a deep tureen
left us by the Luftwaffe.
And all our world in its entire scope
could be contained in crayon
on an envelope.

Lachesis Lapponica

Fatmomakke,
diamond jewelled compass of the north,
always with its needle pointing true.
In Spring the Same come
to live in firewood brush-homes
called *kåtor,* kindling tee-pees
shaped like witches hats.
They trek in closing circles
from Ransern in the north, Kultsjön in the south,
beating tracks for one's imagination
to follow, drawing the seasons to them
as they pass. An old man's hands
thread tin into deer hide,
twist loops through loops until none
contains the other. And only an expert eye
can pin a holding circle to its genesis.
The tourists collect from kiosks
lappish work;
a deer horn knife, or a *kåsa*
to quench the thirst of an afternoon.
But now the cloud
has shaken down the pelt of the Great Bear,
it thickens into life, raises its back,
and scratches at a constant itch
upon an arch of light.

Wolf

Xanthe Hall

I heard him howl in Hungary. But he did not eat me, although I offered myself on a plate deep in the night. My hands in the Finnish forest of his hair, I yearned to strip him down to his pelt and watch his teeth grow. But he kept his clothes on and I kept my decency.

I saw his wolfish smile in Warsaw for the first time a year before. I wondered how a man could look so pleasantly ferocious. He ate all my cigarettes one by one and drank large amounts of beer in the daytime. At night he drank Zubrówka And his eyes never left mine for a second.

We met again in Moscow. I circled around him for hours before I sat down at his dinner table.

Is this place free? I asked, surrendering.

It's yours, he said, gesturing for me to sit down.

Those eyes, that smile.

Even then he kept his paws off me. he let me carry his bottle of Armenian cognac to Vysotski's graveside, where he laid a rose and took a drink with the dead folk hero, pouring a little cognac onto the grave. On Red Square he told me the story of how the Finns and Hungarians parted, way back at a crossroads in Central Europe. He told me the story of the Soviet Union in three minutes. He tipped the bottle of cognac in my dry direction, ever so slightly, and I took a drink. Then I was lost.

He showed me how to drink vodka in the correct amounts so that dancing together flowed from the glass. His smile got larger and I could see that when we were not in one another's arms, he fixed himself to a stable object. He was becoming fluid. His eyes started to flow down his face but the smile remained. And when I kissed him goodnight I sensed that the drink had not killed his appetite but if I ran he could not follow. So I ran.

Little did I know there was no getting away. Thousands of miles between us and you can still reach out and touch me.

If I can't dance to it, it's not my revolution.

And I went home and told my man, my beloved, that everything must change. I took some of that wildness back with me and frightened him with it. I wanted to fall in love with him again, to wipe away the wolf. But he just looked at me with incomprehension in his eyes.

The revolution came suddenly and without warning. My life turned upside down and back to front. A bottomless pit opened up and I fell endlessly downwards, the walls rushing by, nothing to hold onto. Agony that only mothers inflict on their daughters. The brutal slicing through of the umbilical cord by her own hand. She sat in her car on an airfield with a tube through the back and gassed herself. Nazi and Jew all in one.

I wandered around alone in my head, banging at the inner walls. There was no comfort, no release. Only horror and anger. Crying your heart out leaves stains on the bed from the blood. The perpetual whys lead only into a labyrinth of madness and back deep into childhood, both hers and mine. And then the memories start looming in the dark, can't quite make them out. A mother's death sends you hurtling through your own history, from birth to the present, and lets you know what chaos means. No answers, only questions.

And messages sent across the Baltic Sea and back again.
I said to the wolf, here I am, eat me.
And he said, I am a family man.

But I know that deep in the night man becomes wolf.
He said, you are around every corner.

At night I slipped away in the dark and secretly danced with him in my dreams. In the morning I awoke, motherless, my man looking puzzled beside me.

With Christmas came the first crisis. I stayed alone in Berlin and danced in the dark, drugged, dazed. I started to think of destruction. Taking apart the life that I had. Exchanging previous bliss for future uncertainty. Wanting the wolf, not wanting the wolf. Eating my cake and not having it.

Hasta la victoria siempre!

And then the man who had always held my head above water from the moment we met came back. We went on living the life that others yearn for. The messages stopped for a while. I said that things must change, but I didn't know what things. Because everything was just perfect. Too perfect for words.

Months went by. The messages changed into phonecalls with even less content than the messages but longer than the rope we were hanging ourselves with. We began organising a conference together. I watched him bending in the wind like a poplar tree, agreeing with everyone, loved by all. The perfect friend and helper. But I could not trust him, not me, oh no.

The winter was woeful. As spring arrived I broke down into thousands of fragment, like a block of ice sliding off the roof in the first thaw. I cancelled living and lay on the floor in bits. After a while I swept them up and went on as before.

But the meaning of the word *before* was lost to me. I was onstage and I didn't know my lines. The audience looked at me strangely until somebody somewhere said, you need help. The bag of bits burst again and the brush was nowhere to be found.

Days of pacing and waiting for help to arrive by telephone. And finally facing a long thin woman with blond hair who used only the formal *You* and shook hands with a cakey-looking smile, who expected me to tell her how I felt. Bloody awful, I said.

It was a good start, I cancelled everything again.

Two weeks passed of soul delving and depth massage. By then it was almost time to see the wolf again. He called me more or less every day about the conference in Budapest. I could hear him licking (or was it smacking?) his lips in Helsinki. I no longer dreamed of the past but of the future, not a long future but a one-weekend future.

And then we were there. In Budapest. Facing each other so that I could reach out and touch his smile. But I didn't dare. So we had a beer instead.

Well, shall we go? Yes, let's go. (They don't move.)

Hours of beers later we were alone at last and dawn was breaking. We stood in the window and the cruel light showed me that one of his eyes had gone to bed without him. And then he said, I fell in love with you in Warsaw.

The kiss was hard and desperate, tense with fear. And then it became like glue so we were stuck in an embrace that could not find its conclusion. And then he said, I have to work in the morning. So I threw him out.

That was no wolf. That was the family man.

The next day he said, I am an alcoholic.

And I said, no you're not. I know one when I smell one.

When you are hitchhiking, he said, nine times out of ten you open the door and you know immediately from one look who the driver is. But the one time you are wrong, you are as wrong as you can be.

And so we went on drinking. I thought his thoughts for him. Time for another beer, I said, although I didn't really want one. We drank on the street and in bars, in beer gardens, pubs, restaurants, anywhere. I saw how he liked to bathe in the sun. How he liked to eat. And then I stopped drinking for an hour or two to give a speech on saving the world to the Hungarians. For after all, that was the reason I was there. He began to fall asleep in his chair. It was the longest I had seen him keep his mouth shut. Because I was doing the talking.

He made up for it later on. He could talk forever. It was impossible to resist his words whatever they were. In the end I asked him to talk to me in Finnish. It had the same political content but sounded much more romantic.

And then he said, my father died from drinking.

Dead.

The body does not rot.

That was when I heard him howl.

The night got hotter and wetter and darker. The words all ran together into a river of sweat. We walked for miles. Every beer was a postponement tactic. And as the dawn broke again we found ourselves at the same window in the same position, mouths glued together while the birds sang the hallelujah chorus. This time he said he should go, but I said don't. It took longer to get from the window to the door, hours longer. The glue stuck fast. We made no attempt to do anything but kiss. And then he was gone and I was left standing hungry behind the closed door, begging him to come back but not saying a word.

The third night was the same but longer still. After he left, I could not sleep but lay on the bed sweating, waiting for time to pass. After one or two hours I got up and went out. The day was scorching, even at eight in the morning. At the conference, I talked to a man about bears in the forests on the Finnish-Russian border. Another man told me about resolving the conflict in Sarajevo. A third man spoke to me about producing *Waiting for Godot* in San Quentin prison. After a while, I thought I might pass out.

At the hotel I rang him to say I had to sleep for an hour. It would be our last night. I stopped thinking about how it might end and fell unconscious, in a coma, dead to the world.

I awoke to the sounds of bells. The telephone and alarm clock were ringing. I was soaked to the skin. I staggered to the phone and he said, I couldn't wake you up. I was banging on the locked door. He said, I wanted to crawl in beside you.

So we went out again.

You and me and the beer makes three.

But I didn't want to drink anymore. I didn't even want to smoke cigarettes, my oldest passion. I said, let's go back to the hotel. In my room we sat on one armchair together, avoiding the bed. I tried to catch glimpses of the colour of his fur inside his shirt without undressing him. Taking away his clothes would take away the man and leave only the wolf who would eat me.

And then he rolled over on top of me and everything changed. The kiss had more bite and stirred my appetite. I began to salivate at the taste of him. I wanted to throw my clothes out the window and eat the damn birds, bones and all. Most of all I wanted to devour him slowly and against his will.

And then I knew that I was the wolf, not he.

The howl I heard was my own.

He escaped. I was backing him towards the bed and he was pleading to be let go. And I saw he had only been playing. I was still fully dressed and too much of a woman not to be merciful, fool that I am. That was my last chance.

He woke in the morning with a bleeding toe. Maybe I had been sleepwalking.

The Québécois Phenomenon
David Hastie

The Québécois phenomenon is centred around the playwright Michel Tremblay, and his Scottish translators, Martin Bowman and Bill Findlay. This article will discuss aspects of how Tremblay's native patois overcame narrow-minded prejudice and bigoted hostility. Although the article is mainly concerned with the Québécois phenomenon, it is clear that for many Scots writers, and playwrights in particular, the obstacles which have been cleared in the state of Quebec and the city of Montreal concerning joual, are still in evidence in Scotland regarding the use of Scots.

The similarities between Québécois and the Scots are so close that it was little wonder that Bowman and Findlay saw a symbiotic connection between the two cultures. Both have similar hang-ups and problems with old-fashioned and traditional colonial attitudes towards culture in general and language in particular. Themes which haunt the Scottish psyche are echoed in the Québécois; cultural identity, being working class, religion (mainly Catholic in Quebec, Protestant and Catholic in Scotland), sexual identity, community, deracination and cultural impotence. The French speaking population of Quebec is just over 5 million, the same population as Scotland, and Carl Honoré states in his article 'The best playwright that Scotland never had' that

> Both cultures struggled with 'English' contempt, their churches have lionized self-denial and guilt; nostalgia for the rural past runs deep; even the populations are roughly the same size. A strong Scottish community in Quebec merely tightens the bond.[1]

The main point of contact, though, is language, where both Québécois and Scots suffer from similar ambivalences, which, in the case of Scots, still has to be sorted out. As Honoré succinctly points out " . . . the vernacular (Québécois) is loudly touted as a pillar of nationhood and quietly reviled for its proletarian associations". And Michel Boyd in Honoré's article commenting on both the cultural differences between the peoples and the impact of the language stated "Both cultures have been, if not oppressed, then circumscribed. For a Scottish audience, watching a Tremblay play is like hearing your own voice refracted back to you through a prism."

Although Québécois is now generally accepted, this was not always so. Originally known as joual, from the French word 'cheval', meaning horse, Québécois sounded to the cushioned ears of those who spoke International French like the coughing of a horse. It is a hybrid language, a result of French-Canadians gallicising the idioms of their Anglo-Canadians masters. For example, a sweet-talking trapper in the seventeenth century had his tongue 'in fur-wrapped'; now 'enfirouaper' means to attempt to seduce someone. A toilet, once a 'backhouse' became 'écosse.'[2] Tremblay was made to feel embarrassed about joual.

1. Carl Honoré, 'The best playwright Scotland never had', *The Globe and Mail*, 31 October 1992.
2. Alex Renton, 'Real questions in an unreal world', *The Independent on Sunday*, 11 February, 1990.

In common with other speakers of joual Tremblay had inherited a sense of shame about the language. In using joual as the medium of *Les Belles Soeurs* he was confronting the inferiority complex bred by the privileged position of Parisian French and European French culture in Quebec.[1]

The rise of joual corresponded with the rise of Quebec nationalism in the late 1960s, and the major concern of the Quebecers and their traditional enemies the church and the English and French ruling classes. Joual was used as a political tool which highlighted the cultural and social differences between a privileged elite and a marginalised minority. Tremblay's revolt against the accepted classical French with joual, was an explosive assertion of national identity and, quite literally, liberated the language. The term joual has now disappeared in favour of Québécois, and this has now been accepted by the French, who claim that they can understand about 90% of what is being said.[2]

Since the 1960s, when Tremblay started writing, the question of usage, legitimacy and popularising Québécois has had a troubled route, despite the fact that the PQ (Parti Québécois) has successfully managed to exorcise many of the age-old inferiority complexes. It is interesting to note how the critics of Québécois felt, and still feel, about the use of joual, and compare their attitudes with its supporters. Firstly the detractors. Cabinet Minister Gerald Godin, described joual as "a half-language in a half country", and the actress Doris Lussier, who spoke it on a TV family show called the 'Plouffe Family' described it as "a cadaver of a language", and actively and angrily criticised it for years. Her scruples did not prevent her from 'speaking it' on this show for which, presumably, she was well paid to utter its cadaverous consonants and horsey vowels! And the author, Jean-Paul Desbiens wrote a scathing denunciation of joual in 1960. So, what is the attitude now, or at least in 1983, from the year in which these comments were written? Desbiens now says that there has been "a great deal of loss of interest in the whole thing". Laurent Santerre, the University of Montreal's expert on Quebec French says, "It's finished, it's over, thank goodness. People have accepted it", and Michel Prairie, a linguist at the University of Quebec says that, "Quebecers now realize that it is a vital and well-structured language".[3] And even the PQ accept those who still speak correct International French and those who speak Québécois. But most do not care anymore. Leandre Bergeron, who compiles Québécois dictionaries states, "more and more Québécois are refusing to have their language referred to as 'horse talk'. We are moving away from edicts of brute force and towards respect of people's will. Let the will of the people decide what language a living organic community speaks."

Santerre also reflects on the fact that Québécois is very like some of the regional French spoken in the mother country and even certain parts of Paris. And he also supports the view that there are many levels of lan-

1. Bill Findlay, 'Quebec's enfant terrible makes good', *Scotland on Sunday*, October 30, 1988.
2. Richler, 'Off patois', *The Guardian*, February 1990, p36.
3. All short quotations in this paragraph are from Glen Allen, 'Quebecers don't worry about 'joual' anymore', *The Gazette*, Montreal, February 26, 1983.

guage and says, "a living language in a society is very complex at all its levels, and each level is no less than that language at any other level. It would be sheer nonsense to refrain through bias from using careful speech or familiar speech". But there are still detractors who see the popularisation of Québécois as a purely Marxist political tool. One such outspoken purist is the Montreal lawyer Philippe Ferland, who in 1973 gave a 'causerie-choc' (shock speech) which was reported in Canada, Europe and in *The New York Times*. His point was that joual served Marxist ends and was "a language bred in the stables of America", and that because joual is the language of the working class and the poor it is degraded and impure. Denis Rouille, the Commissioner of the Quality of the French Language of the City of Quebec, says disparingly,

> There is the familiar language spoken in the tavern and in the streets by disadvantaged people, little people who don't read. You can't take it seriously. There were idealists who were for 'la langue populaire' but it hasn't attracted people.

Rouille seems to have missed the point. Allen's argument is that people can and should have the choice in certain circumstances which language to speak; English, French, Québécois or all three. The language issue is no longer the *cause célèbre* it once was. For the new generation coming up quickly behind Tremblay and Brassand, language is just one of several means of communicating on stage. It is not a political issue. With a zeal rivalled only by Quebec's newly galvanised business world, performing artists are staking out a path along international cultural circuits leading to fame and fortune in London, New York and Paris. On stage and off, they speak Québécois.[1]

Like many Scots who feel embarrassed about their language, Tremblay is more positive about his Québécois:

> "It's my culture. It's the first language I heard," says Tremblay, who regrets that television and radio are slowly killing joual. He enjoys working with it because, he says, "It uses words in a very lively, colourful way, just like Tennesee Williams and the South Americans. *Les Belles Soeurs* arose from a burning urge. We come from a people that were kept silent for 200 years. I was born being ashamed of who I was and the way I talked. Joual was the vulgar part of Québécois culture. The élite dreamt of going to Paris and being recognised. They despised joual. We were the first generation to say we can stay in Montreal, and talk about Montreal and sing Montreal and still be artists, instead of doing a foreign accent."[2]

Not only does Tremblay write in a non-standard language, practically all his works are set in the same area of Montreal; the east-end working class area of his childhood, the Plateau Mont Royal.

> "When I write, I certainly don't intend for plays to be produced all over the world," says Tremblay. "I write for me and Montreal. When I was younger, I discovered that talking about what was near me was better than trying to be universal. Any writer who writes anything anywhere is universal."[3]

Ironically, it is exactly this ego-centrism and parochial philosophy

1. Marianne Ackerman, 'Sweet Jesus! Who's that, Ma?' *Saturday Night*, June 1988, pp40-47.
2. Renton, 'Real questions in an unreal world'.
3. 'In Person', *The Globe and Mail*, Toronto, 17 November 1990.

which has catapulted him to world wide fame, which seems contradictory
to his dramatic intentions. On Tremblay's philosophy, the writer/director
Jean-Claude Germain says,

> Michel has, and has always had, only one real interest. He is deeply interested
> in himself. His point of reference is homosexual. The given is his family and
> personal experience. He isn't and has never been interested in the larger
> social picture.[1]

This is extraordinary when one notes the effect his plays have had world
wide, including Scotland where the brilliant translations of Bowman and
Findlay show up a symbiotic relationship between the poor east-end
Catholic working-class Montrealers and their counterparts in Glasgow.
But Tremblay's dramatic perspective is very different from that of some
Scottish playwrights still stuck in the realistic/naturalistic kitchen-sink
drama. Tremblay does not highlight at the foreground of his plays the
causes of his characters' unhappiness, such as poverty, unemployment or
homosexuality. Instead he concentrates on the emotional and spiritual
aspects of life. Catherine Lockerbie, commenting on Tremblay's narrow
fictional world, warns Scottish writers to take note "for Tremblay is not in
any sense a cosmopolitan writer. He writes almost exclusively of his city,
Montreal; indeed, of one particular circumscribed area of Montreal and
the vicissitudes of its daily life".[2] Tremblay also takes care not to write
straight-forward realsitic dramas, claiming that, "I will do a lot to avoid
making kitchen-sink drama".

Tremblay was inspired to write in Québécois after he and André
Brassand saw a Quebec-made film which inappropriately used as its lan-
guage "a stilted Parisian French"[3] and "which stopped identification with
the characters".[4] Tremblay and Brassand discovered that they hated the
same things, "the imported French of Théâtre du Nouveau Monde, the
boulevard comedies of the Rideau Vert, the folksy rural bias of popular cul-
ture and the pretensions of the Oútremont bourgéoisie".[5] Indeed the class
attitude and social snobbery of Quebec/Montreal in the 50s and 60s was
so prevalent that one could not stay within the working class milieu and
be an artist at the same time. But, undeterred, Tremblay forged ahead and
wrote a play in the his parent's language, highlighting the Québécers polit-
ical and cultural resentment against French colonisation. Many of his plays
are reflections and studies of confusions of identity, sometimes on several
levels; cultural, socio-economic, sexual and nationalistic. This is amusingly
depicted in his play *Hosanna* in which a drag queen makes his living by
playing the part of Elizabeth Taylor as Cleopartra. The play encapsulates
various confusions over identity, and, of the play, Tremblay says,

> The culture at the time belonged to the people who colonised us. We were in
> the process of asking who we were: were we just a cheap labour force, a sub-

1. Ackerman, 'Sweet Jesus, Who's that, Ma?' pp40-47.
2. Catherine Lockerbie, 'A Prophecy fulfilled', *The Scotsman*, 15 April 1985.
3. 'In Person'
4. Joy Hendry, 'A spinner of quality yarns', *The Scotsman*, 6 July 1992.
5. Ackerman, 'Sweet Jesus, Who's that, Ma?', pp40-47.

species of French? I wanted to write about the problem of identification. I thought that the idea of an English actress living in the United States playing an Egyptian myth in an American movie shot in Spain would be a nice juicy metaphor for Quebec.[1]

Tremblay also claims that he has, "never written one real political play. I think political plays die very quickly".[2] His remark should be noted by Scots dramatists as a warning. Tremblay is right. Explicit political plays based on ideology and, even to a certain extent historic events, do not have the same impact between the time they are written and when performed at a later date. For instance how many revivals have there been of that quintessential political/agit-prop tract, *The Cheviot, the Stag and the Black, Black Oil?* Tremblay writes apolitical plays but has changed a whole country's views over the thorny questions of language, homosexuality and to a certain extent, class. He has also, according to Robert Lepage, director of the Théâtre Répère, explored other areas such as,

> experiments with multiplicities of voices, different epochs and parallel worlds. He (Tremblay) was reacting to a poverty of means in Quebec at the time. It's in this way that all revolutions happen in the theatre. You arrive with an idea because you have nothing else.[3]

How does this compare with Scotland's dramaturgy? We are not in such a desperate situation, yet some Scottish theatre directors are still looking over their shoulders to London, and Michael Boyd, when he was at the Tron, saw this 'Englishing' of Scottish theatre as self-conscious and stultifying.[4] Perhaps this has been the problem with Scottish playwriting as a whole since the end of the World War II. I feel that there has been too much emphasis on the negative aspects of the Scottish psyche and the Caledonian Antisyzygy and an overexposure of the Scots as a downtrodden, unfairly treated people. A handful of Scottish plays, most of them recent, have moved away from the documentary, agit-prop and naturalistic modes, and thus become exemplars of the direction Scottish theatre should take. I am thinking mainly of *Men Should Weep*, especially Giles Havergal's expressionistic production in 1982, *Elizabeth Gordon Quinn*, and *The Cut*, all of which are successful plays where form triumphs over plays with more traditional ideas of content. In neither of these plays are usual shibboleths such as unemployment, poverty or a West of Scotland hard-man image, highlighting how tragic life is for the working classes. Instead there is a real move towards the individuals and motives which is a much more effective way of expressing the state of the human condition. What Tremblay has done successfully, which most Scottish playwrights have either ignored, or failed to do, is to exploit the use of metaphor, and only a handful of Scottish plays to date reach anywhere near Tremblay's achievement. Tremblay dislikes the term 'political play' anyway, and instead prefers to call his dramatic and prose works 'fables'.[5]

---

1. 'I write for me and Montreal', *The Globe and Mail* (Toronto), 17 November 1990.
2. Findlay, 'Quebec's enfant terrible makes good'.
3. Richler, 'Off patois', p36.
4. Alastair Cameron, 'Boyd in the Hand. An interview with Michael Boyd', *Theatre Scotland*.
5. Findlay, 'Quebec's enfant terrible makes good'.

It is ironic that Montreal's Le Théâtre du Rideau Vert, a traditional theatre which specialised in boulevard classics and middle-of-the-road drama, put on *Les Belles Soeurs* in the first place. Co-founded by an east-end Montrealer, Yvette Brind'Amour, whose own working-class accent has been modified by long periods in Paris, it was instrumental in the 60s in opposing the Quebec government's plans to encourage local playwrights. The story goes that Brind'Amour staged the play as a way to prove that experimental theatre by young, trendy, left-wing, nationalistic playwrights was a total waste of time. The success of the play, and of Tremblay's reputation since, has proved the detractors wrong on all counts.

The sensation of the first night of *Les Belles Soeurs*, on 28 August 1968 almost caused a riot in the audience more used to Parisian French. It must be remembered that the audience were subscribers of the theatre, as there is little, if no, public subsidy for Canadian theatre. Such was the impact of the play that a movement began which called itself 'the theatre of liberation'. Despite his success, Tremblay was, at least up until 1985, still censored on Canadian television.[1] At the time, and for a period afterwards until the dust had settled, purists and traditionalists accused Tremblay of mere sensationalism by mixing gutter talk with art to produce results.

"A talented dramatic writer possessed of extraordinary gifts of observation", wrote La Presse critic Martial Dassylva. "However, considering the coarseness and vulgarity of his play, I can't help but think the Rideau Vert has done him a disservice by agreeing to produce it."[2]

Tremblay concentrates on marginal people on the periphery of society who struggle for legitimacy, identity, love and most important of all, a voice. At the time this article was written, Tremblay, at 45, is Canada's most widely produced playwright. His output includes 20 plays, 8 novels, 5 screen-plays, 7 translations/adaptations, plus pop song lyrics and film and opera criticism. His plays have been translated into numerous languages and dialects, and have been produced in Scandinavia, South America, Italy, Japan, Scotland, England and the USA, as well as Canada.[3]

To elevate Michel Tremblay to the heights of sainthood may be exaggerating things a little, but it is not far from the truth as far as reactions to his plays in Scotland are concerned. Here are only a few of the epithets which have been written about him. He is described as a "folk hero", "a touchstone", and there is talk of a "Tremblay phenomenon". His plays are described as "gritty tales of hurt and laughter in working-class Quebec"; he is "a boon to Scots theatre abroad", and that "he has become an icon of the Scots language renaissance". Supporters also talk of "his gilded niche here", (in Scotland). And Michael Boyd's first reaction to the Bowman/Findlay translation of *Les Belles Soeurs*, (*The Guid Sisters*), is positively ecstatic, "I was stunned by the daring marriage of sophistication, surrealism and naturalism. It was like a lungful of fresh air".[4] *The Guid Sisters* has

1. Lockerbie, 'A Prophecy fulfilled'.
2. Ackerman, 'Sweet Jesus! Who's that, Ma?', p40-47.
3. ibid
4. Honoré, 'The best playwright Scotland never had'.

become one of Scotland's most performed plays since the seventies, which surely must be a worrying aspect for Scottish dramaturgy. Scotland has simply failed to produce a single playwright with any of the same credentials.

But for all Tremblay's success in supporting and championing Québécois, the Canadian-English translations have fared less well.

> In English, Tremblay's plays reveal little of the colour, resonance and musicality of the originals. The gap is present in the very first words of *Les Belles Soeurs* – "Misère, que c'est ça? Moman!" becomes "Sweet Jesus, what's that? Ma!" The curious hint of black American slang leads nowhere. For the most part Tremblay's translators, John Van Burek and Bill Glassco have gone for a homogenised often literal rendering of the language – about the level of service one could expect from headphones at a Pequiste press conference.[1]

The above article was written before Bowman and Findlay brought out their Glasgow/Scots translation in 1989, and prophetically Ackerman states that "a less literal, more poetic rendering of joual into cockney, and Irish brogue, or black American English might at least communicate some of the richness of Tremblay's language."[2]

If plays written or translated into Scots have had difficulty in England, although to be fair most of the productions which travel have been very well received, then Québécois language plays have had an even more difficult time in France, and Paris in particular. Ironically, and to some of the more conservative thinkers, inappropriately, Tremblay has won the Quebec-Paris literary prize at least twice; in 1984 and 1985. This has a parallel with a situation in Britain where, to the disgust of many, James Kelman won the 1994 Booker Prize with his novel, *How Late It Was, How Late*.

Scots therefore has worked more successfully as a target language for Tremblay's plays than either Canadian or Standard English. Both Québécois and Scots are mainly urban, short on vocabulary, punchy, aggressively pronounced, hyperbolic and often profane. They are also, because of historical developments, extremely witty, in many cases, non-intentionally. And Findlay states, "By translating Tremblay, we wanted to show Scots dramatists that the vernacular need not constrain, that it too can be combined with experimentation and ambition."[3]

Tremblay also employs a dramaturgy which is familiar and loved by Scots; a populist working of the plays, and a sense of the burlesque, music hall and vaudeville; in other words a synthesis of popular and traditional Scottish theatrical conventions which, at times can be unashamedly sentimental. In fact *The Herald* critic after seeing George Gunn's *Songs From the Grey Coast* urged the author to go and see how Tremblay handles movement and the audience in *The House Among the Stars*.[4] And on the success of language as a spur to recognising national identity, Boyd concludes, "We have, in a funny kind of way, exchanged true portraits of ourselves. And that always helps you to feel that you exist that much more".[5]

1. Ackerman, 'Sweet Jesus! Who's that, Ma?', p40-47.
2. Ibid
3. Honoré, 'The best playwright Scotland never had'.
4. John Linklater, 'Oor sorrows must an oor hearts find,' *The Herald*, October 26, 1992.
5. Bill Findlay, 'Talking in Tongues', *Theatre Scotland*, 2, 6 (Summer 1993), pp15-22.

Gerrie Fellows

Tableau

The walled garden of her childhood

became   in another country
open   undulant ground
a place of hollows and hill slopes

(How many ways there are to slip through it
as gently as a ghost from childhood
revisiting paradise)

From its beginnings in flame and sawmill
the farm edged back the wild
The orchard was planted with apple trees
pear   French walnut the vegetable garden
set with rows of potatoes
pumpkins   the silvery stems of beet
In the washhouse among the baskets
and the bulbs stored for autumn
an old Manx cat gave birth
to a lineage of stub-tailed kittens
Okuti had become a familiar map
of paddocks   kennels   woodshed

In the garden my grandmother began
to create a living geometry
daffodil silk at the edge of the orchard
mauve anemones and the multiple heads
of the polyanthus
waxy shining platefuls of azalea
velvety nemesias, long spike-leaved ixias
African marigolds the colour of egg yolk
nasturtiums twined crisscross over gravel
the blue hydrangea

The calendar of plantings
became swathes of colour, scent, texture
As elaborate as etiquette the garden stirred and bowed
each beautiful head to another
the massed glories of the floral dance

She held the bush at bay   without fences
with the delicate acquisitions of empire

The garden was a pattern and a ritual
a way of approaching perfection

Into it she sank anger loss shame
her own pain and the pain of the letters which came:
Frances miscarrying while her husband drank
and Helen in Africa
what was told between the lines of her letters
what her life was
could not be spoken of   She buried the grief of it
Only her brother was happy
playing the stock market and letting his fine mind
run to seed in Sunningdale

Was she   the youngest, her father's darling
the only one to have learned his dictum
that work makes us
that without it we are nothing?
Her siblings fought him   They thrilled to occasions
her sister-in-law making an entrance
in furs and diamonds
But this was what she wanted   to live in her body
simply   in the open air

It was true
she never quite got used to the country
its lack of deference, the informality   the accent
But she did not want to go back
She bit her lip   and clipped the heads of the roses

And years later
from the carved desk in Bay View Road   refusing
to visit us in England   she did not write
it's more than forty years, it's another country
but   the garden would go to ruin.

*

On the visitor's gate my grandfather carved the name Arrochar

As he sauntered down the slope of the lawn at dusk   (the day lily
blooming and closing itself up)   the wooden gate opened

to a mythical territory: something ancestral he kept in his name
a motto above a compartment wavy
Not a place   a heraldic field.   Not the incised leaf of the oak
or the feathered leaf of the matai   but a shape
as formal as a playing card   a spade on a cloth of tartan

Nothing real   Nothing we needed now.

*

My grandmother woke in the night
hearing my mother's sleeping feet glide
out of the french doors of the bedroom   across the veranda
crunching the milky quartz pebbles of the path
silently crossing the dewy lawn

a morepork calling   the stalks of the bamboo shifting and scraping
the feathery edges of the bush   its greeny shade calling
stem and creeper, stalked green
the mossy tumble of the water
the creek's song to the myriad speech of the bush
the scuttlings of small creatures, screeches scurrying
growth of roots   leaf surfaces

There is way of moving
out of the hem of the moonlight into the bush
footfalls almost quiet   you pause   your eyes
grown used to the dark
There is a way
of stepping out from the heraldic flora of empire
and stepping into leaf vein   deep pools of water over stone

Listen

The people of the place are here before us

There is a way of passing through the bush
of coming to stand at the edge of the lawn at night
observing the cut borders   the heraldic flora of empire

There are other voices

There is a way of listening

*

A footstep on a track down a hill slope at dusk   (the day
closing crumples itself up)   The gate opens

to smoke blowing over the stacks
two herons, leafless birch   But this
is a photograph from another decade   another country
What is not recorded   are the danger signs, a territory
a warhead   metal beneath a compartment wavy

*

What is not recorded
might be as simple as a portrait from 1940
my grandfather in his gumboots in front of the cowshed
Perhaps he dreams there   early morning, his face
already turned to shadow   the photograph evaporating
and his heart like clockwork.   It's machinery he loves:
Give it to Mac, the neighbours say   He'll fix it.
He knows he's not much of a farmer   but hell,
he's a good Kiwi   he can fix anything
except the farm   and his own life. He muses there
alone at the edge of the garden with the gate
into which he has carved the name Arrochar
so that it will open out into everything:
two herons   leafless birch
a photograph his granddaughter will take in 1990

In Egypt in the Great War he found an alabaster head
in Surrey he found love   He is only forty-seven,
surely   he can still make something

*

Dear Mrs Macfarlane,   It is with very great sorrow
In the dry dock   the plates of the hull
In his room   a fallen beam

There is so little one can say

She turned the soil of the garden   It was almost winter

except that he died in the service of the Empire

She buried her anger deep in the ground.
She ran the farm.

*

Constance Geraldine Macfarlane 1893-1977

Her name and the dates of her life are a plain inscription on a boulder set above the bare yellow paddock of winter grass where she most lives, where her ashes were scattered, where for years she'd set her jaw and grubbed the gorse in obstinate struggle with the soil and the colonising, tenacious shrub it harboured.

From here the house is a square tin roof nestling between the fold of the hill and a finger of bush. We go down through the yards at the back of the woolshed. Ramshackle fences, everything at different angles, askew. The spaces of childhood diminished rainlashed but still magical, like a peeling shadow.

I go down in fear of the alsatians I know are there (old childhood phobia). For strangers live here, incomers with city dogs. I go down knowing I carry the past, like a cup which spills from the hand onto what is: this neglected house in rough grass, gardenless. My grandmother's transitory flamboyant art a nostalgia of fluttering colour.

All she has kept buried has been set free by her death. It grows under the house, cracks its foundations, swells and splits its grey weatherboards, sloughs off the window sills. The house is a family pod burst open to show the bastard inheritances of disapproval, resentment, denial. Generations of the family idyll that said you cannot be yourself. Disappointment, the refusal of love.

Listen. There are other voices. Other angers lift the house. Angers from the time of acquisition (eighty thousand acres, a bargain at two hundred pounds). Angers from the time of division: the arcadian dream out of the burnt ground. In the twenties Kai Tahu from Wairewa worked as casual labour on the Pakeha farms: it was the natural order. For was it not the coming of the Pakeha which gave the land its value?

The gate carved in my grandfather's hand opens to childhood journeys (the heady garden, the couched valley) and the journey we make now: the loaded southerly opening out over the flat at the head of the lake: Little River, Wairewa. No, not many Maori here now, my uncle says as we drive through. These days most of the houses are second homes for people from town.

CENCRASTUS

The Quarterly Magazine Covering Scottish and International Literature, Arts and Affairs since 1979

ISSUE 59 - AVAILABLE IN LATE JANUARY

Featuring:

An Interview with Bernard Mac Laverty
'Murdo Comes of Age' - new story by Iain Crichton Smith
Scottish Education Under Examination
The Knoydart Land Raid Remembered
Why Scotland No Longer Takes Holy Orders

COMMENT ❖ POETRY ❖ FICTION ❖ REVIEWS

UNIT ONE
ABBEYMOUNT TECHBASE
EDINBURGH
EH8 8EJ
TEL/FAX 0131 6615687
e-mail:cencrastus@dial.pipex.com

Also Available from
CENCRASTUS:

'Two Clocks Ticking'
Poems by Dennis O'Donnell

'a true poet' *Iain Crichton Smith*

'an articulate Scot, worth listening to' *Alex Salmond MP*

Ghost Dancing

Susan Castillo

The moment I set eyes on her, I know this woman will bring me nothing but trouble. Why, I really can't say. Perhaps it's the way she stands, feet apart, knees slightly bent, as though preparing to fell an unseen adversary with a fatal karate kick. Her hands are jammed into the fringed pockets of a worn suede jacket. Her hair seems to have a life of its own, and crackles with indignation. On her fingers are several large and rather gaudy silver and turquoise rings. For some reason, I remember my mother's dismissal of a girl I once knew as 'the sort of person who wears a ring on her index finger.' This woman is planted squarely in front of the display case containing the Ghost Dance Shirt, grimacing and muttering to herself.

We often get visitors who are a little strange, especially on weekends. Sunday afternoons are the worst. We see all kinds, faded old ladies with blue hair and battered woollen hats, seedy unshaven men with empty eyes who smell faintly of liquor, crazed suburban housewives with raucous children in tow. My Collection – I call it mine, though in actual fact I am only its Curator – seems to attract more than its share of this sort of visitor. Perhaps it is because anything to do with Indians seems appealing and exotic for people who lead drab lives. The old women can dream of dashing warriors who will sweep them off to the forest. The men can fantasise about submissive squaws, or about going on the warpath against obtuse bosses. The mothers smile as they think of sinking a tomahawk into the skulls of their noisy children.

This woman is, however, not the usual sort of visitor. Her eyes are feral, dark, vaguely Oriental. She stands straight and tall. I move closer. "Neocolonialist bastards!" she mutters. Heads are turning.

Clearly, we cannot have obscene language in the Museum, with so many children around. There are security guards to deal with this sort of thing, but for reasons I can't explain I move closer. "Miss?"

She is oblivious. She stares at the Ghost Shirt and continues her diatribe. "Assholes!" This really can't go on. I touch her elbow. She spins around.

I put on my blandest, most unctuous smile, guaranteed to calm trustees, society matrons, visitors, and other raging beasts. With this woman, it has no effect whatsoever. "Who the hell are you?" she spits out.

"Well, actually, I work here. I'm, er, the Curator for North American artifacts." For some reason, I am blushing to the roots of what's left of my hair.

"Oh, yeah?" she sneers. "Then I suppose you're responsible for . . . *this!*"

"In a manner of speaking. This is one of our most popular exhibits. It has belonged to the Museum since 1890, when it was sold to us by a translator in the entourage of Buffalo Bill's Wild West Show. We're quite proud of it. It's one of the few Ghost Dance shirts in Europe, and it's really in excellent condition. May I ask what brings you to Glasgow?"

She looks at me through slitted lids. Then, suddenly, her attitude undergoes a change. She crinkles up the corner of her eyes, grins and sticks out her hand. It is surprisingly warm. "I'm Lorne Lone Eagle from Oklahoma. I'm here doing research at the University."

Lone Eagle? Aha, I think. "I'm Percy Crichton-Shaw. You have an interesting surname, Miss Lone Eagle. Is your background perhaps Native American?"

"Yeah, I'm part Cherokee, part Plains. What did you say your last name was?"

I repeat, "Crichton-Shaw", but Lorna laughs and says, "God, what a mouthful. Can I just call you Mac? All you Scotch are supposed to be Mac-Something."

I don't particularly like this, but one can't be rude to a lady. And I find Lorna Lone Eagle intriguing. Up close, she is really striking. Curiously for one in my profession, I have never had much contact with Indians. Perhaps this is my chance to have an Indian friend. So I reply, "Why not?"

She looks around. "I would kill just now for some good strong coffee." I hear my own voice saying, "Well, I can offer you some from the machine in my office, Miss Lone Eagle." Perhaps she will be impressed when she sees my mahogany desk and my two telephones.

"Lorna, please. Sure, Mac." She walks along at my side, silver bracelets jangling. As we leave the hall, she glances back over her shoulder at the Ghost Dance shirt, but a ray of sunlight slanting through the west window has turned the front of the display case into an opaque gold square.

After my secretary serves us coffee, we chat. I am normally not the most forthcoming of individuals, but I am astounded at how much I seem to be talking. I tell Lorna how my interest in Indians came about when I was small, how I had always been fascinated by the Western movies my mother disapproved of. I tell her how I used to buy American comic books when I was sent away to school in England at the age of seven. Lorna reacts in horror. "At *seven*?" Well, yes, I say, and explain that people from my sort of background always go off to school quite early.

"So that's why you don't sound like you're from Glasgow." She looks at me pityingly. "!That's what they did to kids on my reservation. We were shipped off to boarding school in Kansas, and they didn't let us talk Cherokee. They said speaking English was the way to get ahead."

I am somewhat taken aback. This is a novel perspective on a public school education at the finest institutions in Britain. But I go on to tell Lorna how I had read Art History at Oxford, how I had advanced in the museum world, how I had established myself as an expert on Native American artifacts. I explain how I have built up the collection here at the Museum, by acquisitions, by bequests from local citizens, and by taking advantage of what the Museum had hidden away in its vast basement storerooms. She asks me what I think of *Braveheart*. I reply, not much, which she finds strange, given my taste for Westerns. When I say I fail to see the link, she shakes her head impatiently and says that both Scots and Indians are always filmed dying in picturesque fashion. But then she shrugs. "At least Mel Gibson looks pretty in his blue and white warpaint. Maybe my ancestors should've mooned the US Cavalry." I launch into a long rambling speech about the tradition of Scots as romantic victims in literature. Suddenly Lorna interrupts. "Mac, are you married?" she asks point-blank.

"Well, no, I stammer. "I live at home with Mother."

"Are you gay?" The interrogation continues.

"Of course not. I mean, at school, everybody was, but no, I'm not gay." I take a deep breath. I'm not used to such directness. Before I can compose myself, Lorna looks at me through her eyelashes – which I can't help noticing are remarkably long and dark – and asks, "Mac, why don't we go out to dinner this evening?"

We spend hours over our meal, talking until the candle on our table glimmers low. Lorna tells me that she's been reading in the tabloids about Devolution, that she doesn't really understand how it works or what it's all about. I explain about the new Parliament in Edinburgh, how it is such an exciting time to be Scottish, how there will be increased control over local affairs. Lorna retorts that it looks to her like window dressing. She says that London is giving us the illusion of control over our own affairs, but that basically the only significant power the Scottish Parliament will have is to raise taxes, which will in turn go to subsidise corrupt politicians who will sell out to the English. She draws unflattering parallels with the Bureau of Indian Affairs. I protest vigorously, though I fear that despite her lack of sophistication she is voicing opinions with which many might agree. I remind myself that one cannot expect a Red Indian woman, no matter how pleasing to the eye, to have a genuine grasp of matters of such complexity.

We discuss the Ghost Dance Shirt. I ask her why she had seemed so agitated earlier on. She looks me in the eye. "Y'know, Mac, these things mean a lot to my people. My dad's family were Cherokee, but my mother's folks were Oglala Sioux, and for them the Ghost Dance was a sacred ritual of hope. I wonder how you would feel if the robes of Mary Queen of Scots were put on display in an American theme park for tourists to gawk at. Those guys who took back the Stone of Destiny had the right idea. If you let people mess around with your past, you won't have much of a future." Her arguments are interesting, but I can't keep track of what she's saying. My eyes are fixed on an utterly enchanting mole on her left cheek.

Lorna and I end up after dinner at the Pied-à-terre, one of the most fashionable discos in Glasgow. When she suggests that we go dancing, I manage to disguise my dismay quite well. I am really not very good at that sort of thing. But I have discovered that in this type of establishment, no-one really watches what anyone else is doing. I have perfected a sort of propeller movement, hands bent sharply at the wrists, arms held close to the sides, scissoring up and down. Lorna, however, is amazing. She dances with wild abandon, perspiring, hair standing out around her head. At one point she leaps on the platform, writhing and flailing, eyes flashing. It is

evident that she isn't wearing a brassiere. She looks into the distance, div-
ing, swirling, bending, prancing to the rhythm of a drum only she can
hear. A strobe transforms her movements into an old movie reel, a jerking
sequence of stills, a ghost dance all of her own. I've never in my life seen
anything quite so erotic, and at the same time so completely innocent. The
stockbrokers and stockbrokeresses who surround us are transfixed, and
step back to form a semicircle. When the music stops, they burst into
applause. I suddenly am aware that most of the male yuppies in the Pied-
à-terre would give a great deal to be in my shoes. I puff out my chest, and
escort Lorna to the door amid envious glances. With horror and delight,
I discover that I am hopelessly enamoured of someone who Mother
would consider totally unsuitable.

When I drop Lorna off at her respectable bed and breakfast (not, to my
chagrin, the sort of establishment where one could be invited in for a
nightcap), I realise that I have learned very little about her. I ask how long
she plans to be in Glasgow. She smiles and says she's leaving for London
tomorrow.

I know that I cannot let this woman get away, that if I do so I shall regret
it for the rest of my life. "That's a pity. If you were planning to stay a bit
longer I could probably let you have a private viewing of the Ghost Dance
Shirt. Or even," and I take a deep breath, "another item in the collection
whose existence very few people are aware of."

"Well, Mac," she says, "that's real nice of you. Maybe I could make a few
phone calls. I'll get back to you tomorrow." With that , she goes in without
a backward look.

The following morning Lorna rings me at the Museum. "I've managed
to fix it with my London friends. When can I have a look at the Ghost
Dance shirt?" I look at the phone and try to conceal my exultation. I prom-
ise to show it to her that very evening, after the Museum closes.

At night, the Museum is eerie, full of echoes. I open the case containing
the Ghost Dance Shirt. It is made of dun-coloured leather, creamy and
soft, with painted crescents in patterns of turquoise and coral. As Lorna
touches it, her eyes go flat and distant. She looks up at me. "I thought this
would be better. I've seen loads of imitations back home just like it." I
know this can't be true, but I am eager to impress her. "Well, there is some-
thing else, something really amazing, down below."

This is something I have never shown to anybody. I couldn't believe it
myself, when I came across it years ago in a dusty basement storeroom
full of Victorian effluvia. Yet I lead Lorna down to the basement and
switch on the lights. "Voilà!" I say.

Lorna draws closer, as though she cannot believe what she is seeing.
In front of us is a woman, standing upright, dressed in Plains Indian cos-
tume. Her skin is yellow-gray, stretched tight over her cheekbones. Her
lips are drawn back from her teeth, in a snarl. She is standing, arms open,
on a wooden plinth, on which a label is affixed: Rebecca Storm Cloud.
Buffalo Bill's Wild West Show. b. Dakota 1830 – d. Glasgow 1890. The

empty sockets of her eyes are black, full of darkness.

"Dear God in Heaven," Lorna says softly. She stares at me. "You poor creepy bastard." Her voice is shaking. In it is not only incredulity and horror, but the unmistakeable sound of fear. The basement is dark and full of shadows. The thought that at last a woman--and not any woman, but a desirable exotic one like Lorna – is taking me seriously makes my mouth go dry and taste like copper. I feel strong, manly, dangerous. But, after all, I have always wanted an Indian friend. I strive to reassure her, tell her that she is in no danger from me. I try to explain that Rebecca Storm Cloud is the Indian friend I never had as a boy, that I like to come down here and look into her face and dream about saving her from bands of marauding cowboys who could never understand or appreciate the purity of the vision of those sightless eyes.

But Lorna, unlike Rebecca, is quite capable of saving herself. She shakes her shoulders and shrugs off her fear as though it were a moth-eaten fur coat. Paying me no attention, she sinks to the floor and sits cross-legged, rocking back and forth, moaning, humming a strange tuneless song that makes my flesh crawl. I realise that it is an Oglala funeral chant. Finally it comes to an end.

I see to my horror and chagrin that tears of fury are rolling down Lorna's cheeks. I sit down awkwardly at her side and take her hand. "Bastards," she hisses. "I heard of cases like this. An aborigine woman who was stuffed and put on display by P T Barnum. The body of an African tribesman exhibited in the Folk Museum of Vienna. God *damn* it, Mac!" Suddenly she is beating her fists against my chest. I hold her close. "How in hell would you feel if you went to a museum and saw a stuffed Highlander?" she spits out, between sobs. I pat her shoulder gently. She looks me in the eye, clearly reaches the conclusion that I am not manly and dangerous but rather middle-aged and somewhat pathetic. Finally, she fishes in her bag. I presume it is for make-up, to repair the ravages of this storm of emotion. Suddenly, however, she pulls out an Instamatic camera. A flash lights up the gloom as she takes a shot of Rebecca Storm Cloud.

"What are you doing, Lorna?" I ask in alarm. "Just a little memento of my visit to Glasgow," she answers. The look in her eyes dares me to make an issue of it. I realise that it is late and there will be hell to pay if the Director finds me here. Lorna looks at me with what seems a curious mixture of compassion and contempt. "See ya, Percy. Thanks for everything." I realise that this is the first time that she hasn't called me Mac. Paradoxically, I do not find this at all reassuring.

The following morning I receive a letter. The letterhead states that it is from Lorna Lone Eagle, Attorney for the Oglala Nation. In it, she says that if the Ghost Dance shirt is not promptly returned to the Oglala Sioux, certain newspapers in America and Britain will receive the photograph of the stuffed body of an Indian woman which is currently languishing in the basement of a Glasgow museum. She adds that it would be unfortunate if the reputation of the Museum as a rational, humane, caring institution were to be called into question. An unsigned hand-written note accompanies her letter: "Dear Percy: When will we indigenous peoples learn once and for all that losing is never beautiful or romantic. You guys had your Clearances, we had our Trail of Tears. It didn't get us far, did it? Losers are just losers, whether we're Scotch or redskins. Maybe at last our respective tribes will learn to fight to win. At least I hope so. Your Indian friend." I know when I am beaten. I shall have to persuade our Director that repatriating the Ghost Dance shirt would be a masterful PR gesture, that it really isn't such a valuable piece, that he could be photographed handing the shirt over to the Oglala, that it would give us valuable publicity, tell the world that we're not a bunch of cowboys. The scrap of paper harbours the faint scent of Lorna's perfume. I hold it close, and imagine I can hear the clicking of her heels on the marble floor growing fainter as she walks away.

Ian McDonough

The First MacHine in Space

Boys, it was something
And it was nothing.
Silent as a pine-wood
Blacker than the Corrie-Dhu
On a moonless December
Cold as a manse.
Damn the bit of smell.

Boys, the earth was a midge
On the face of Ben Badh
And a cloud of suns
Hung like stags' breath
In the iron morning.
A kilt of stars
Bound it all together
In a pattern
A man could read forever
And never find the match.

Boys, what was it like?
The longest sermon ever penned
Delivered in an unknown tongue
To a congregation of the deaf
In an echoing prison of a church
Without a floor or walls or roof.

MacHine Heaven

It is a languid, liquid Tuesday afternoon
With nothing to do till a year on Monday
On a hillside a piper plays a half-familiar tune
Haunting a glen which teems with friendly ghosts.

A scent of burning whins permeates the air
Keepers and Collietrons have been cleared to Australia
No-one can remember the Prime Minister's name
But everyone can remember all of 'Flower of Scotland'.

Money is considered an indelicate thing at best
And is confiscated from tourists at the border
Though since the Visitor Centre was burned down
They are scarce, and generally of a quieter sort.

The glen's chief export is, in fact, chiefs
Who are sold as soon as they display any leadership qualities
In return, the glen receives supplies of a rare exotic weed
Which is ingested as proof against the Calvinist Flu.

It is forever a languid, liquid Tuesday afternoon
The waterfall is tinkling like ice-cubes in a glass
Darwin, Marx and Freud are buried and forgotten under grass
A few MacHines have started swinging through the trees.

Three Games of the Clan MacHine

Eleven of the clan pursue a sphere
also pursued by eleven Keepers.
The sphere is charged
with a powerful symbolic intensity.
It is also charged with a magnetic force –
The Keepers wear large magnets in their boots.

At unpredictable intervals,
in order to decide a pre-arranged issue,
a gathering of the clan and Keepers will occur.
Keepers stand to one side,
observe the clan do battle with itself
and return home, having secured a standing majority.

When two or more of the clan are gathered,
they are prone to speculate
on whether an unconfirmed, invisible presence
is coloured green or blue.
This game is dogged by frequent injury.

A MacHine Enters the Virtual Forest

Masts of fibreglass and pine: the resins weep into fine worm-free
ground.
See yon far cut-glass mountain glinting underneath a UV sun?
It crawls with static virtual mountaineers, precipitating
phantom avalanches with their tongue. Inside the air-conditioned glade
a corporate hermit tinkers with his life-support machine, adjusts
his intravenous drip of sugared barley-bree. He scatters hazelnuts of
wisdom to the squirrels for a reasonable fee.

And round the virtual forest-paths the virtual tourists run, averting
perfect virtual eyes from needles littered round the forest floor. The
Keep
of Heritage (admission virtually free) plays tapes of pipers forging
virtual notes, and sells authentic forest muck to fresh-faced scholars
keen to blacken up. Deep in the braveheart of the inner wood,
a carbon-fibre cross flashes its runes and shows an endless video
of ancestors who slew their Gods to live inside a waking state.

Why the Clan MacHine Abandoned Accountancy

If twenty comes
And twenty goes
Make forty wents
And wents
Are one pound each
We will be rich
But have no time
To hunt the stag
Or linger
On the beach.

A New Life

The man whose clothes I stole
is running naked
through the back streets of my brain.

He is shouting at the top
of my voice . . . "I will get you,
you thieving bastard."
But knows that only he and I are listening.

I have some surprises in store
for the naked man.
Soon, heavy snowshowers

will begin to fall, and the wind
will get up a little. Naturally,
it will emanate from the north.

Why am I so mean to him? Why
are my streets so cold,
so charmlessly bereft
of the milk of human kindness?

Because these garments, garish,
preposterous, outlandish, gauche,
have wrapped themselves
so tightly round my bones,
I tear and tear
but cannot rip them off.

Border Ballad

The moon, which borders
On a state knowing no reason,
Swings over mountains with impunity.

Swings between coyness
And a lusty streak across the sky,
Falls drunk into the hissing sea,
Gets itself arrested by the dawn.

Gets itself banned
From the Cartographic Society
For changing the names of its oceans
Into a language of static interference.

The moon, which glows like treasure

But is larded up with dust,
Beams a cheesy smile on midnight ramblers,
Licks the bare backsides of lovers.

Cares not a jot that some big toothy grin
Has stuck a flag into its skin.
Or that it is judged a harsh mistress
By the soft and mistressless.

The moon has a voice so low
It opens your bowels, breaks your teeth,
Shoves your astral readings
Where the sun will never shine.

The moon borders on a state of mind
Without the hindrance of a mind.

Ghost Broadcast

Donald S Murray

It was after Archie found the wireless in the remains of the old shop that voices began to return to his home.

They hadn't been there for a long time. Not since his parents sat up in their beds over twenty years before and whispered about how their younger son might not manage to get by without them. Not since his father prayed in the sitting-room, his thoughts slipping back to the days when Archie's brother, Andy had been alive. Not since the times when the house echoed with old songs and ghost stories; the surge and dip of voice and music from the Home Service and Radio Eireann on the wireless set in the corner of the shop or sitting-room.

But the day he limped indoors with the old radio in his hands changed all that. He discovered it in a tea-chest where it had been packed away for years. He brushed clear the cobwebs draped across its surface, wiped clean the dust on its dark Bakelite cabinet. Using spit and fingers, he scraped off the dirt obscuring the names 'Athlone', 'Hilversum', 'Moscow' on its dial. There was a wide grin on his face as he did this, remembering how people used to come to the house and try to glean news from its whispers. Times had been good then.

So good that there were evenings when Archie believed he could catch sight of these days in the sitting room mirror. He would be sitting down in the fireside chair and, looking up, discover it was still occupied by someone else. His mother, perhaps, who had died in 1962, her knitting needles still in her hands as they had been that afternoon her head had dipped, surrendering to death . Or his father who had passed away in 1959, reading the Bible as he had been when he shuddered and died. And all around them, their surroundings would be just the same as they were today. The chest-of-drawers in its position at the back of the room. The faded red curtains, rosy with daylight. The framed inscription reminding visitors that 'Christ is The Unseen Guest in This House'. Only the electric light was new, replacing the tilly lamp that once lit the room's shadows.

Underneath his parents' gaze, Archie set to work, spending his evenings with the radio's bits and pieces scattered like a huge mechanical jigsaw on the table. He would weigh each valve in his fingers, wondering if it might work. Each coil and spring would be blown clean of dirt. It was a large Ekco radio – made in 1933 and worked by batteries – and they had lumbered with it from the shop into the house each evening. He giggled to himself as he remembered his mother's outrage that spring evening in 1938 when his father brought the wireless home.

"*What on earth did you buy that for?*" Mam had asked.

"*It'll bring us custom. People need more than a wee cat's whiskers to listen to at times like these . . . They'll come to us for their food and an earful of the daily news.*"

Dad had been right. They would arrive at the shop, using the excuse of a quarter pound of tea or some cheese or sugar to listen to the daily news bulletin. '*This is the one o'clock news from the BBC Home Service...*' As he put the wireless back together, he could hear the voices of that time, see the faces of the villagers in the old mottled mirror as they crowded into the room to hear Neville Chamberlain speak of "*a quarrel in a far-away country*" or how he had gained "*peace for our time...peace with honour*".

It was as if he were watching an old film. He could recognise the people – Margaret Ellen (died 1956); his brother, Andy (lost at sea, 1942); William (1963) – but it was as if they were moving through water. Their expressions blurred and indistinct, they made their way across the room like people waking after a long sleep, uncertain of how much they could rely on their own bodies. When Archie went to bed that night, he wondered if his dead relations and neighbours would ever return again to his home. The effort of imitating gestures that had come so easily to them while they were alive seemed such an impossible strain.

Yet they were back again the next day. Old Alasdair (1949) and his wife, Annabel – who had outlasted him some twenty years or more – were restored to their usual chairs. His head was bowed when the newscaster announced that all those who were members of the Royal Naval Reserve should enrol at their local depot. He muttered a few indistinct words – something no doubt about his own experience during the Great War. Archie remembered he was always going on about that.

Annabel, however, was more interested in the songs of the day. She would hum along to the music of Vera Lynn, sing;

"*Love and marriage, love and marriage
Go together like a horse and carriage . . .* "

in her high and tinkling voice, yet at the end of the evening, her large, plump body would give a little shiver of disgust at the hours of sin she had just enjoyed. "*They're nothing like as good as our old Gaelic songs,* " she would declare as she headed out into the night.

A moment later, he heard his mother's voice. He glanced upwards to see her face – more lined and paler than it had been while she was alive. Andy stood before her, patting her shoulder with little, jagged movements of his hand. He was dressed in his Naval Reserve uniform, a tight knot of curls peeking underneath his cap.

Archie knew what this moment was – the day his brother had been called up. Washed and featureless, his parent' faces had none of the emotion they displayed back then. It was as if they were only responding to a faint memory of that time, repeating words they had long forgotten.

"*You're the young man of the house now,*" Mam had said.

"*Our wall against the storms of old age,*" Dad muttered, barely troubling to conceal the sarcasm that was in his voice.

Archie went out for a few days after that, risking the mockery of children shouting 'Drool' and 'Knucklehead' after him as he limped down the village road. He made his way to the Post Office, to vans which delivered bread or fresh fish. Once or twice he managed to pay a visit to people of his own age long stranded in their homes. They would ask him questions, astonished at the way he could recall the dates of particular events, especially when they considered how slow he was at everything else. Yet in places like that, he had to make an effort. Shave and wash before going. Say a few words in conversation. It was all so much easier to stay at home and switch on the wireless.

If he did that, he could hear the broadcaster's voice pronouncing names – like Hitler, Stalin, Mussolini – that had been unfamiliar to them before his wireless came. The words of Winston Churchill, telling his people that this was "*their finest hour*". The mocking tones of Lord Haw-Haw with his "*Jairmany calling. Jairmany calling.*"

People would come to visit him too. Cousin Marybell (1953) would sit, aloof and proud as she had been in life, her face more chilly than ever as she eyed with disgust the rim of mud and cow-dung that still clung to the heel of Allan's boot some thirty years after his burial. Death didn't seem to suit him as much as some of the others. His former, rosy colouring had fled his face, and he seemed a little ridiculous without his usual shade of skin.

He knew to what they were listening. The names of the ships that had been sunk by the enemy over the previous week or so. Many of the village-lads were on these vessels, whether as part of the Royal or Merchant Navy. His brother was on the 'Consul'. Annabel's boy, Angus on the 'Annique'. Margaret Ellen's nephew, Murdo on the 'Preston'.

A woman wailed as the name of one ship was announced – Eilidh whose eldest, Roddy was on the 'Helen'. He saw her body crumple as she heard the news, the others rushing to comfort her . . .

He listened, too, when 'Lord Haw-Haw' announced Dundee had been destroyed by German bombs. The villagers' eyes fixed on one of their number, Margaret Ellen. Her son worked in a factory there. Her hands became clenched as she sat there; her knuckles whitening.

"*We don't know if it's true,*" she announced.

The others continued to stare at her, horrified by the thought that Donald might lie dead alongside hundreds of thousands of their fellow country-men and women in that city of jute, jam and journalism.

"*After all, it's Hitler's cronies telling us this,*" she said, her voice brisk, calm and logical. "*It doesn't have to be true.*"

Defiant in her disbelief, she left the house, her heels rocking as she did so. When she returned some ten days later, she was clutching the letter Donald had just written triumphantly in her hand.

It was the following month that grief became a permanent lodger in the household.

His father began to grow more focused as that day approached. Archie could make out once again the few wisps of grey hair on his otherwise bald head; the little, lop-sided mouth; his tight, near-sighted eyes. He could even distinguish what the family had for dinner on a particular day:

the skeletons of herring stretched out on a plate; a lamb-bone whittled clean of meat; the inevitable pile of potato peel. There were times when he was so tired of his own cooking – the continual use of the frying pan, the fish boiled free of flavour – that he wished he could reach into the mirror and pick the remains of his own plate.

And of course, there was his mother. He could see her thin, gaunt features; the dark shawl wrapped around her shoulders; her tiny birdlike nose; the way her fingers tapped out their own message of alarm as the news came to an end and the list of missing vessels was announced.

"His Majesty's Government regret to announce that the following vessels have been reported lost or missing at sea: 'HMS Wesely'; 'HMS Pauline'; 'HMS Consul, . . ."

There was a gurgling sound from his mother's throat, as if breath had been denied her and she gasping for its return. She stood up, reeling, and a moment later, Dad was also on his feet, making for her, trying to hold her in his hands.

"Oh, God . . ." he said, *"Why this son? Why this son?"*

He held her as she stumbled towards the mantelpiece. Archie could see his father's face as it pressed against the mirror, distending and distorting on the glass. His nose was flat and white, as if he were trying to escape the time he lived in and shove his way through to the present day. His mouth drooled saliva, white spray dribbling to the bottom of the glass.

"Why him? The child of my right hand?"

As he mumbled, the others in the room gathered round his parents. He saw his mother embraced by the dead; brave Margaret Ellen wrapping an arm round her trembling body. He saw his father being drawn away from the mirror; the stains of breath and grief left behind on the glass. William had already started offering a prayer of comfort.

"A Thighearna, thoir dhuinn cuideachadh . . ."

For the first time too, he saw himself – a poor stunted boy who sat in the corner of the room. *"Da . . ."* He tried to reach his father, but his words and step were far too slow. He turned towards his mother, but the bodies of others blocked his way, crowding round her. *"It's too soon to give up yet. Remember there was that fellow the other day who was discovered a whole week after his ship went down,"* Margaret Ellen assured her.

Finally, someone reached out to give him a comforting hug. He thought it might have been Annabel, but when he looked into the mirror to confirm this, already the identity of his long-dead relatives and friends had blurred.

"Put it away!" he heard his father's muffled shout. *"Put that thing away!"*

And he could see himself, moving towards the wireless at the back of the room. He did then what he must have done all these years before. He switched off the set to prevent its voices from reaching his home.

Tomorrow he would put the wireless back inside its box.

David Nicol

Rig yird

Hard plantin amang chuckies an boulders.
The heid rig is a soss wrocht by coulter;
sliddery grey watter swillit airn cleuk seuch.

The ribs o Ben Faw lig knappit an stark,
dry as tombstanes upon sun-cuikit clay.

Sparks flee as blade skeeters aff rig back,
dirlan spade grip, ditheran airm.
Als caller and snell a wind bleeze
caas larch fra the haund.

Peat rig

Saft in the skimmerie grund
the blade snoovis hame
swashan whisky dyed watter,
airn spade in dark pool
atween peat cleavit waas.

Spruce happit in yird wame:
stem chappit by haund,
buit ding drave ruit in,
gien a yank tae mak siccar
she's snod.

Canty she birstles
on lithesome sough at my back
as I stap atour peat rig,
tane pace on tither
tae mark the neist plantin.

Gowk storm

Hail sweeps the glen as a besom,
chillan the brae
whair I faa til my knees
dang by wind blatter.

Happit wi tree bag
I culd only squatter
in peat furrow
as a puddock
until watter ran
ower my buit hem.

Cauld flesh on weet plastic.
Bidan my time
for the rain tae blaw by,
in my heid I am runnan
wi friends doun Ben Faw:
Hurl open the Gordon Arms door.

Birk

Up in the heichs
abune pleuch gore
the burn splairges
siller amang birk.

Strunty they grow
in the craig,
hunker frae
sheep nibble
an frost.

Drumlie I swither
in bud brakken bower
efter scoffan my piece;
in a dwam
I plant visiouns
o birk forest.

Guddlin

Aff wi the gloves!
Andrew caas
as we lade out
the spruce
wi bare haunds,
grippan thaim
in bundles;
the preenack scarts
bluidy our airms.

An row up
your sleeves man.
Lat thon insecticide
breenge throu your veins;
it'll haud back
the midges
whan we gang guddlan.

Plantatioun

In night ingyne green brae visioun
is mingit wi whit paper:
lines peyntit wi pleuch
cryan out for a screiver
tae mak words on Ben Faw.
Awan nocht but a spade I plant ALBA.
Nouther by pen dicht nor yird scart
I dream a new natioun wroght wi pine trees
flourishing reid amang bud bristan larch.

Splitting

Samantha Coleman

On the table is a finger. I keep looking at it, I can't help it. The thing that fascinates me about the finger is the nail. It's painted red but the paint is chipped. It's been chewed at and the skin around the nail is hanging and looks sore. Well I guess it's not sore because it's not connected to the person any more. But I don't want to think about it.

Somebody once said that sometimes the skin around a nail looks more appetising than a meal. I think it was an old boyfriend that said that.

There is a trail of blood from the finger to the door, not a straight trail but a frantic one. One that sprays and diverts. There is blood on the door. Bright against the white paint and smeared around the door knob. I pick at the chocolate cake that's on the table. The cake was a treat for myself, I would have liked someone to share it with. The finger lies next to it. I could have shared it with the owner of the finger.

I should tidy up, get rid of the finger but somehow I can't move. I feel drained. Ready for collapse. The fight's gone out of me. I've fought enough. Fought to keep my job, and when I lost it fought to get another. I'm ashamed to admit it now but I lost my job because I had a temper tantrum. I'm not very good under stress and believe me, I was under stress. I threw books and papers around and generally made a mess of the place. I enjoyed it while it lasted. In my own world whilst I created a whirlwind of paper, paper clips, pens and pencils. Then I stopped and realised everyone was staring at me and that I was crying and screaming. I'd lost my temper and as a result I lost my job and spent the next few months watching daytime TV. Which is enough to drive anyone mad. There's only so many cookery tips, fashion tips and how to get your man tips that a person can take.

Going to the job centre was degrading. The men in their torn jeans, smelling of sweat and loafing around. The women with their bright red lips and their 'can I help you' patronising smiles. Reminding me of my sister, the sister I haven't spoken to in about five years. We never got on as kids. She would bully me, boss me around, made me a nervous kid. Now she has her own bossy kids, and a neat little husband with a neat little house.

When I was fourteen I met a girl who I could really talk to. She was my best friend. She wasn't interested in boys and make-up like all the others as they paraded around in their tight jumpers showing off their little boobies. We didn't have boobies. Flat as ironing boards. No hips either, just skinny. At the weekend we'd go to the park. We'd sit on the steps to the women's toilets. I remember the smell of urine and disinfectant.

"Blow a smoke ring," I'd say. It always fascinated me as she made her lips into a perfect O and out would blow a ring of smoke. Sometimes we'd play the spitting game. Who could spit the furthest.

She liked to set fire to things. I'd help her gather leaves and old newspaper, squatting beside her little pile she'd try to light it. I'd see the excitement in her face at a small orange flame. Often it went out. Then she discovered paraffin. When I heard that the school had been set alight I knew who'd done it. That was one fire that didn't go out. They say that it blazed for an hour until fire fighters got it under control. Apparently the head of the school was on his knees praying to God whilst the flames ate at his school.

I hate religious people. They bore me. They are so fulfilled or they think they are. They come knocking on your door and ram their opinions down your throat. They don't listen to a word you say. Nobody ever really does.

And what would happen to them if you took away their God? Who would they lean on? They have forgotten how to rely on themselves. Not like those of us who have always been alone. We have to think for ourselves. We are surrounded by people but we are completely in our own heads. Occasionally we have a short conversation with the shop keeper or the lady at the bus stop about the weather. Nothing really important. We walk through a busy street, are brushed on all sides but are surrounded by ghosts. But religious people think they can knock on your door and become your best friend in an instant. Like earlier, there's this woman knocking on my door. And today I haven't been feeling on top of the world. You know, daytime TV getting to me. This woman, she's wearing the perfect face. Perfectly made-up, perfect clothes, shoes. I answer the door in my old jogging suit and my dog-eared slippers. I push back my greasy hair. She reminds me of one of the job-centre women I told you about.

She starts on about sin. She tells God to forgive me, standing there in her perfectly unladdered tights. And like I said, my hormones are playing up or something but I invite her in anyway. I haven't had visitors in a long time. She sits at my table smiling, with her Bible on her lap. She says to me, "God will forgive you of your sins". She smiles and I start to hate that smile and all it represents. Her upper-class background that gave her her good shoes and clothes. And I knew that she felt I was nothing. She could see into me. What was I doing with my life? Nothing. And to do nothing is to be nothing.

I ask her what she classes as a sin and then I say wait, don't tell me. And I go into the kitchen and fetch the cake that I'd been saving for a sinful moment. I bring it in on a plate with a knife and stick it in front of her. "Do you class that as a sin?" I ask, indicating the cake. She smiles and gently says, "No, I would class adultery as a sin. A cake is a cake". "Adultery? I haven't slept with anybody for five years. Do you think anybody would have me?" I smile at her. She looks a bit worried by the way the conversation is going. Maybe she thinks I'm a psycho. I tell her that the last man I slept with left a ten pound note on my kitchen table and crept way into the night.

"Now, do I look like a whore to you? Do I look like a Mary Magdalene?" I laugh at my own joke but she's not laughing. She's standing up saying she has to go. But I don't want her to because I don't get many visitors. So I say, "Here have some cake". Pointing at the cake with the cake knife. And she just stands there staring at my chocolate cake like I've poisoned it. This pisses me off. I was just trying to be polite. Always the way with these stuck up people. They are so uptight and ignorant. Anally retentive.

So I think to myself, who is this woman that she can come into my house and lecture me about sin, and then stare at me like I'm alien. God, some people have some cheek. And I find myself getting really mad. And then I feel that whirlwind coming and the lady disappears.

And now I feel exhausted and the lady really has gone. Only she left her finger behind.

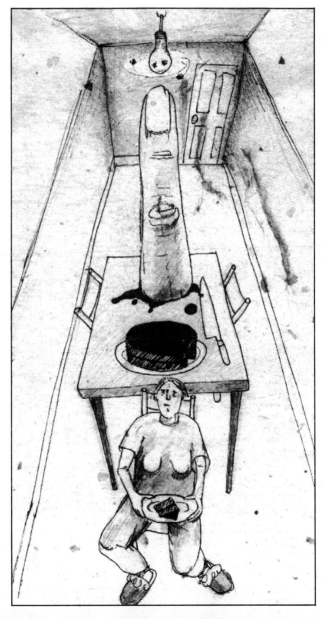

Illustration by Hazel Terry

The Hour-Glass Woman

Samantha Coleman

Teresa waddled when she walked on account of the extra layers of fat on her stomach and legs. Her eyes, lips and nose disappeared into her round squashy, sweaty face. When naked her belly, breasts and buttocks hung down. She looked into the mirror in the bathroom and tugged at her layers, perhaps hoping they would come off in her hands, perhaps admiring them. She wore huge dresses of purple and red that attracted people's attention.

Nobody liked making friends with fat people, unless you were funny and fat and then no one took you seriously anyway. So Teresa preferred it on her own. She lived in a block of flats, ten floors up, on the edge of town. She kept her curtains closed. After all, if she looked out of her window there was nothing to see apart from gangs of bored youths hanging around getting drunk on cheap cider. If her window had faced south she would have been able to see the sea. Teresa loved the sea and how it smashed against the cliffs. Crashing, foaming, breaking. Her flat was covered in pictures of streams, rivers and oceans. She had sculpted statues everywhere of women with protruding bellies, women with spears, women with pear-shaped breasts, all in deep brown earthy colours.

Anybody respectable never drove around this end of town. At night music pumped out of car stereos. The youths made fires in metal bins and across the street was a run down hotel with a broken red neon light that flickered into Teresa's bedroom all night, turning it into an empty nightclub.

She was fascinated by all the freaks in the world. To know that not everyone was perfect made her feel good. Just think, people were born stuck together – babies with two heads on one body. She was fascinated by tiny people, huge people. When she first watched *The Elephant Man* she was saddened and horrified. She watched the film over and over. Someone else had been persecuted for not being perfect. She didn't mind too much that people stared at her or when kids called out to her. She was used to that, and she liked the power she felt to know she was not like the other people.

One group of kids were particularly cruel. They'd been hounding her for years, even ringing her up and taunting her down the phone. She would get pictures of nude fat women through the letterbox. The women were always in obscene positions with some kinky instrument in their hands. She knew who had sent them. She imagined the boys climbing up the ten flights of stinking stairs, giggling. On Teresa's bad days this got to her. She felt angry, she wanted to kill. Instead she'd get out a tub of ice cream. She knew who the leader of this gang was. She'd seen him hanging round the house with the others. It seemed the others looked up to him, followed him. He had started throwing things at her and then the others followed.

About this time he and a few of the others started having dreams about Teresa. One sticky July night the leader dreamed he was being chased by a giant snake. It had Teresa's face. He ran until he reached a swimming pool. He jumped in but Teresa followed. He couldn't swim and was drowning. Teresa was laughing at him. The water turned to sand and filled his mouth, his nostrils, his lungs. He woke up sweating. He didn't tell the others about his dream, even when he began having it night after night. Another boy had a dream about Teresa too. In this one Teresa was a green lizard-type creature. She had a huge long slithering body and was slithering towards him as he was tied down. She slithered right over him and began to crush him. He couldn't breathe. The boys forgot the dreams in the day.

Most mornings Teresa waddled off to the local supermarket and most mornings the boys called out obscenities to her. This morning the group of boys began to shout out at her, "Hey Fatso, you want some chocolate?"

The other boys laughed and began to waddle down the street after her. Teresa ignored them. She was breathless and sweating by this time. The boys began to follow at a distance all the time calling out to her.

When she reached the supermarket she carried on walking. They followed. She walked out of town. Past the old railway tracks, past the rubbish heap that stank and was haunted by diseased cats with gammy eyes. The boys had stopped shouting now but continued to follow. Soon they came to the beach. Walking through sand was hard for Teresa. The boys followed silently wondering what she going to do. Their over-active teenage minds worked overtime. Would she drown herself? Drown them? Where the beach became narrower there were caves. Teresa walked to the caves and went into the blackest deepest one. Here the boys hesitated. Should they follow? But what would the fat lady do, she was too fat to be dangerous.

Inside the cave Teresa had sat down on a jutting rock. She waited for her heart to slow down. She waited for the boys. She remembered when she was young and larger than everyone at school, nobody wanted to be her friend. She stood alone at the edge of the playground watching the others play. She wouldn't eat school lunch with the rest of them; instead she would wait until classes started and then would go into the cloakroom with her bag full of chocolate bars, crisps and cakes and eat until she felt sick.

She remembered when she found a book on power and magic in the library and her body disappeared, no longer important. What became important was the power of the mind. She found she could be whatever she wanted to be. She could have an hourglass figure if she wanted to.

The biggest and bravest of the boys came first, the leader. As his eyes grew accustomed to the dark he began to scream at what he saw. On a jutting rock sat a half woman, half snake. A woman with hissing serpents crawling out of her head. The woman was huge, she slithered towards him and as he screamed again she glared at him. She turned him into stone and with a flick of her tail turned him into sand. He crumbled to the cave floor. Another boy came forward and peered into the cave. He saw nothing only heard what sounded like the rattle and hiss of snakes. He backed off as his dream came to him. The boys ran off.

Whenever Teresa went shopping the boys only stared at her, half in fear, half in respect. Occasionally she gave them a snake dream to think about.

'Three Craws sat upon a wa" (A critique)

Angus McFarlane

Three craws sat upon a wa'
sat upon a wa', sat upon a wa'
Three craws sat upon a wa'
on a cold and frosty morning.

The first craw wiznae there at a'
wiznae there at a', wiznae there at a'
The first craw wiznae there at a'
on a cold and frosty morning.

The second craw got up and flew awa'
got up and flew awa', got up and flew awa'
The second craw got up and flew awa'
on a cold and frosty morning.

The third craw fell an' broke eez ja'
fell and broke eez ja', fell and broke eez ja'
The third craw fell an' broke eez ja'
on a cold and frosty morning.

This poem is one of the neglected greats. But its cultural provenance is not the only reason for its claim to greatness. I will closely argue why it deserves greater recognition. At first, the poem presents the reader with a deceptive simplicity, but beneath the surface there is a vibrant sub text that makes 'Three Craws' Universal.

Initially, we are drawn to the fact that there are three 'craws'. And, of course, the figure three alerts us to a fundamental aspect of Western religious belief. Foregrounded is the mystery of the Godhead: three in one, one in three. To further emphasise this, the 'craws' are anonymous: they are not given individual names. This means that they are One in their anonymity, although decidedly three in number. The paradigm is clear. Their anonymity reminds us of the mystery of the Christian God, of an impenetrable cosmic identity that we cannot know. But the Platonic other-world of Forms is suggested too. The namelessness of the 'craws' implies that they all partake of one thing, Crowness. They are poised at the brink of the empirical world, yet break the boundaries of sense to become a Universal Form; an example of feathery 'gestalt' in a world of Ideas. Furthermore, the pre-Christian, Pagan world is also configured through the figure three. The Christian story of the Crucifixion tells us of three men on crosses. In the Pagan, pre-Christian era it was believed that people could be turned into birds and animals through the power of magic. And if you were tacked up on a cross you'd want to be turned into a bird too! The subconscious desire of the three crucifees to fly away, if I may refer to them as crucifees, is strongly suggested. Indeed, the poem is criss-crossed with allusory strings that jangle quite a few bells when given a sharp tug.

Freudian theory of the subconscious invites the comparison of the 'wa"

Illustration by David Schofield

in the poem with a barrier of some kind: a barrier in the mind, perhaps, between the conscious and the subconscious. The 'wa" reaches out to us as an irresistible Freudian metaphor, a metaphor that represents many images of separation; as in the division of the Id from the Ego, the Berlin Wall that divided East from West, the Great Wall of China that divided the Chinese civilisations from the encircling barbaric hordes, Hadrian's Wall that kept the Picts from the Romans, the Wall of Death in a travelling fun-fair that separates the bike riders from the gullible punters, Pink Floyd's 'The Wall' that used to divide the hip from the unhip – and any other wall you care to mention. Anyway, the point is that if you think a wall in a poem is just a wall . . . well, you're crazy.

There is also an association with death, of course. Any poem worth its salt has one somewhere. Crows are associated with death through our superstitions. Their colour, black, is the colour of mourning. And the fact that it is a "cold and frosty morning" reaffirms dark thoughts of death. Once again, Pagan belief provides further elucidation: the 'cold and frosty morning' connects our thoughts to Winter and the death of the old year. And so we have it; metaphors, images, inferences, suggestions, hints, skif-fies, nods, winks, meaningful looks and blethers: all provide a plethora of ways to understand why this poem deserves a greater reputation.

However, it is the second verse that really elevates 'Three Craws' above the ordinary. The first 'craw', we are told, has no physical existence. In fact, it never has had one. We are told it "wiznae there at a'". Nevertheless, three crows have been posited in the first verse. Suddenly, we are referred back to the initial intimations of a Platonic world of Ideas. This metaphysical image is arresting in its power to surprise and intrigue the reader. It is all the more impressive when one is reminded of Cartesian doubt. It's easy to imag-ine a kilted MacDescartes pondering if he 'wiz' or 'wiznae there at a'". Being and non-being, cosmic angst, Brigadoon and Buddhist belief that the world is merely an illusion are chucked into the mix. Heidegger's concept of 'Dasein' is sloshing around in there somewhere too, I'm sure. Furthermore, it is a sign of our rich heritage that this poem should have been set to 'music' and sung by raucous crowds of Scots who have drunk large quantities of alcohol. This way of expressing our culture lends the poem its vatic quality, a Dionysian characteristic that informs the listener that our past is kept alive in poems passed from generation to generation by drunken griots swigging bottles of Buckfast. It connects us to an immanent Caledonia Mundi.

The second 'craw' leaves. Hence the saying, to the shoot the craw; meaning to leave. It is a mark of the poem's complete integration with the Scots tongue that some people use this saying without knowing its origin. One must also remember that we speak of going to one place from another without deviation – as the crow flies. But try telling Virgin rail that.

The third crow introduces a human aspect to the poem. And this is where the meaning of the poem begins to unravel. We are told it fell and "broke its ja'". But we know that crows have beaks, not jaws. To reinforce this example of personification the three crows 'sat' on the 'wa". Birds would perch, not sit. And so the breaking of the jaw and the sitting on the wall gives the crows a more human aspect. And for what purpose is their Crowness undermined by this attribution of human characteristics? What underlying meaning is the poem leading us to inexorably? At this point the hidden meaning bursts to the surface. The crows are, in fact, the three crucifees! One leaves, Christ, and flies directly to heaven. The other two are left; one to ponder the non-existence of a phantom bird while nursing his broken jaw.

So, if anyone still thinks that 'Three craws sat upon a wa" is merely a nonsense rhyme without a shred of significance, they should think again.

Of course, we must be careful not to exceed the bounds of literary analysis. This would render a critique valueless. It would also make the critic in question look like a complete tube. What I mean is that a poetry analysis should know where to stop. Some of the young Turks in Universities nowadays would go far too far because they're egotistical bastards angling for a research grant and want to impress nubile undergrads so they can get a shag. They would probably waffle something about the crow flying off to figure in another poem that mentioned a crow. They might say it went off to be the crow in the poem by Ted Hughes, 'Crow Alights'. We are then faced with the surreal image of a crow flying from one poem to another. Not only that but we're forced then to accept that when it alighted on the window sill in that poem it came eyeball to eyeball with Ted Hughes as he smoked a fag and drank a mug of tea while staring out of his window at dusk. The idea that an example of an object in one poem, qua object, could migrate to another poem is clearly ridiculous. The words 'daft' and 'brush' spring to mind. I mean, how could the bird in 'Crow Alights' get back to 'Three Craws' in time for someone reading that poem from the beginning? The poem would instead read, "Two craws sat upon a wa' because a third had buggered off to be in a Ted Hughes' poem". See the problem? Wouldn't scan. Things, qua things, just can't be in different poems at the same time. And how crazy would people think we were if we thought this was possible? Imagine, there you are, walking down the road with your kids when one of them points to the clacking V shape of geese in the icy sky. "Look dad," one of them says in wonder, "aa they geese. Whaur they goin'?" And you say; "Oh they're probably just flyin' fae one poem t'another." You'd be locked up.

But if by any chance such an insane idea does gain currency in the wacky world of literary one-upmanship. I hereby claim the right to say I thought of it first. Paws off! Anyway, my conjecture that one crow is Christ flying off to Paradise is much more credible, don't you think?

Lastly, it is highly significant that the poem has no single author. However, its origins from a Landseer-like misty past make the poem politically relevant today. Our Scottish Prime Minister would be proud of a poem that is truly a 'people's poem'.

Editor's note: I had the idea of writing a piece along these lines many years ago, but failed to translate the idea into reality and Mr McFarlane beat me to it! Rats!

MacBeth's Social Worker

Angus McFarlane

Duncan the Meek's little known plan to spread PC awareness among his warlike Thanes in the 11th century failed. The following extracts from the recently discovered diary of a social worker sent to MacBeth's castle, Heather MacBlether, shows some of the reasons why this happened. We also learn how far off the mark Shakespeare was in his 'historical' dramas.

25th June 1040

Brill! I'm off to MacBeth's castle tomorrow. Looking forward to the challenge. Case notes are a fascinating anthropological record: husband fights wars, wife stays at home. Both young and ambitious with an eye for the main chance. And I see they're childless, but want to start a family sometime. Mmmm, could be a problem. 67.8% of Thanes die in battle or are murdered. Still, sperm can be easily frozen in this climate until the widow is ready.

27th June 1040

Settling in, but my room is rather Spartan. Walls running with water, coarse matting on the floor and spiders in the straw mattress. A couple of pitch torches for light – which've left soot rings on the ceiling. Never mind, a few deft feng shui touches here and there and the room'll vibrate in harmony with my inner being.

Warmly welcomed yesterday by the Thane and his wife. (Just call me Big Mac, he said.) Lady M is super too. Smiled sweetly and said everyone'll become PC pronto or she'll cut their balls off. Mmmm, no need for an Assertiveness Course there then.

1st July 1040

Norway has invaded! Castle hoaching with shaggy haired warriors. Messenger woke us all before cockcrow. Hammered on the gate. Old gatekeeper took ages to answer. Could hear MacBeth yelling, "Git yer thumb oot yer erse an' open the fucken gate, ya dickheid!" Couldn't help thinking a stress management course would help. Must teach him to negotiate personal desired outcomes. Useful event, though. It's given me an idea to write another 'Lifeskills' piece. 'Loud knocking and how to cope'.

28th July 1040

Alba's won! Norwegians defeated – although that's no cause for triumphalism. King's coming to stay tonight. Preparations all day for royal banquet. Hens' necks wrung, wild boar's throat cut. Yuugh! Up to our ankles in mud, blood and feathers. Suggested to her Ladyship that a vegetarian meal washed down with highland spring water would be a good idea. Just smiled sweetly. Asked how long madness had run in my family. I was a bit taken aback. Confessed I had a couple of weird sisters. She stopped plucking a broiler and gave me the strangest look. Said she'd have to see to the evening's entertainers and hurried off. (Wandering techno-bagpipers and a line-dancing troupe. 'The White Heather Clubfoots')

By the way: Lady M dropped a letter from MacBeth in her hurry. Noticed that he'd written 'Norweyans' instead of Norwegians. Oh dear, dyslexic then.

29th July 1040

Murder! Uproar! Treason! Duncan's dead. Murdered by guards. A bad hair day for Alba. Had to begin post-traumatic counselling right away. Amid the din and confusion following the discovery of the King's body I offered counselling to anyone who needed it. Lady M cried out, "Eh need t' hae a blether" – then broke into floods of tears. Two minutes later she was smiling sweetly. Said she felt much better. Amazing! Counselling really helps those in deep, psychological pain.

2nd August 1040

Drugs in the castle! Hallucinogens! A stable boy stopped me today. Winked. Asked if I wanted to have "a good time". Smiled slyly. Produced some pills. Said they were made from "root of mandrake" dug up at midnight. Known as 'mandies', he said. I said I'd tell MacBeth. He laughed. Said Big Mac was his best customer! Now I understand the strange goings on in the dead of night.

When relieving myself in a dark corner the other night I saw MacBeth flit past a torch in the courtyard. Foaming at the mouth. Gibbering. I heard snatches of words and more. "Murder", "daggers", "tak them back yersel'", "D'ya think Eh've got a zip up the back o' ma heid?" – and then something about Alba's need for a proven striker in the six yard box. Then he's up to the moonlit battlements, howling, "Glamis hath murdered sleep". Poor Lady M. Her husband's already dyslexic and a druggie – and now he's developed an elective lisp.

16th August 1040

Feng shui re-organisation of my room goes on. Helped, would you believe, by the stable boy. Brought me a shovelful of horse shit mixed with straw and soaked in urine. Wonderful abstract shape. Lends itself to various interpretations. A gift from Lady M apparently. (Must thank her.) Decided to ask the boy at what point horse shit, piss and straw becomes Art. Eye of the beholder, etc. . . He says, "What if the beholder's a warhol?" I says "Y'mean asshole". He says, "Same thing". But despite a few misunderstandings, we're becoming friends. He's begun to confide in me.

Said he overheard Big Mac talking to three underclass figures. Seems as though Banquo's to be murdered. MacBeth's best friend! Unbelievable! Psychotic behaviour brought on by abuse of mandies, no doubt.

25th August 1040

Jings. Crivvens. Help ma Boab. Banquo's been murdered. Body found in the woods. Stabbed dozens of times. Stable boy says everyone suspects MacBeth. But some good news. Fleance, Banquo's son, escaped. Fled abroad, probably. What a shame. He was so looking forward to Higher Still.

Another banquet last night. But big trouble. Broke up after an 'I spy' game went wrong. Apparently MacBeth cheated. Something beginning with 'B', he said. Battle-axes, beer, beards, boar and bonding – as in male – were all turned down. Then MacBeth yells "Banquo" and stabs a finger in the direction of an empty chair. Cries of "wanker" and food flying. So MacBeth proceeds to trash the place. Very pissed-off. Thanes took to saddle and went home early. MacBeth's drug problem is really getting out of hand.

7th September 1040

Could be that MacBeth's nearing the end of being in denial. Met him stumbling through gloomy castle passageways. (On my way to counsel a milkmaid who'd knocked over a pail of milk). He mumbled something about my 'weird sisters' and magik powers. Said he'd heard I knew strange words, like 'anal retentive', that could induce sudden, deep sleep in anyone. Also, that I'd used words to transform a shovelful of horseshit into a work of everlasting significance. Then asked if I could help him.

I decided a negotiated needs analysis would be best. He wanted to know if his throne was in danger. And were all fouls fare if it was a Rangers player putting the boot in. I said we'd negotiate an agreed answer. He mumbled something about there not being simple answers to simple questions in the black Art of Social Science.

3rd February 1050

Success – after 10 years of counselling. Have discovered the root of sorrow for MacBeth and Lady M. He did murder Duncan. He admitted it. And Lady M had a hand in it too. But, naturally, it wasn't their fault.

He was abused as a child. Uncle gave him sweeties then assaulted him. So, when Duncan rewarded him with Thane of Cawdor, it was another figure of authority handing out a present. That triggered suppressed memories of childhood, feelings of loyalty mixed with unconscious desire to rid himself of the representative object. But not only that Lady M told him the king 'resembled' her father as he slept. Suggests Electra complex – daughter sexually attracted to her father. Unbearable feelings of guilt when Duncan appeared. Result. Both wanted the symbolic figure killed for personal reasons. So, there you have it. All explained. That should put an end to that simplistic nonsense about killing someone for naked ambition alone.

Sheena Blackhall

Devolution: The Open Door

On the 11th day we treetled doon,
Tae makk wir merk, the voters o the toon
Nae firey cross tae set the warld ajee
A scrat, jist pencilled in. Syne, hame tae tea.

September '97. Fine gairdenin weather,
Fowk scalin frae their wark began tae gaither
At pollin booths in Nellfield, Northfield, Nigg . . .
Seeven hunner' year afore at Stirlin' Brig,
Wallace tuik tyranny, an thrawed its thraipple.
A secunt bite, thocht I, at yon same aipple –
O self-determination . . . Nationhood . . .
(Oor Past's preserved, *preserves!,* bi Hollywood)
Setterday Bravehairts at the fitba match
The Flooers o Scotland dinna play – they watch.
A puckle luikers-on . . . bit at yon poll
We got tae kick the baa, an score a goal!

I waukened on the Friday. Yon wis rum.
Jist ae lane seagull skreichin on a lum
Nae pipe band's cheer. Nae Common Good bunfecht.
Nae gun salute, tae show we'd got it richt
A queer hello, tae Devolution's daw
A bittie in the Press, an yon wis aa.

Twis like a moose, trappt bi a muckle steen
That lowsed, can scarce unsteek its captive een . . .
Sae fooshunless, uneesed tae Liberty
It canna grasp the aim o bein free.

Setterday, tho, the Mither Kirk gied voice
Wi peals o bells that we micht aa rejoice
Her grey doos rang a paeon frae their reest
Frae thon great belfry at the civic breist.
Their clangin, unsnibbed Jubilation's gate
Let Celebration in . . . a thochtie blate.
While far ablow, an elder liftit up
The siller glory o a haly cup
Studded wi pearls, a treisur, lang concealed,
Thon day o days, it shone . . . a gem, revealed.

Like this, oor kintra. Ancient, is the line
Far firey Celt & Viking intertwine

Hid bi the shadda o a neebor-lan
Times turn. In risin sunlicht, noo, we staun

Destiny's flittin ooto Number 10.
A new door's openin. *STEP BEN! STEP BEN!*[1]

Twa Futterats

Twa sleekit futterats in a waa
Commenced a conversation
On fit Reality sud mean
A dyke, their illustration.

'A dyke's a hideyhole' quo they
'Far we may hide frae sicht.
A camouflage . . . a masquerade . . .
A screen. A cloak that's Heaven-made
Oor prey tae nab bi nicht.'

'Yer wrang!' a moosie pypit up
'This steeny bouer's ma hame.
A bield, tae hoose ma furry clan,
The littlins o ma wame'.

'G'wa!' (The corbie gied a skreich)
'A dyke is bit a reest.
A perch tae park ma feathers
Fin the pech gaes frae ma breist.'

A fairmer, stottin frae a howf
Anetth the sickle meen
His spayver lowsed, an jubilantly
Stoored agin the steen.

This stopped the futterats' learned claik
Their pheelosophic leanins . . .
Twa hummlit, drookit, wycer breets . . .
The truth his mony meanins.

---

1. On 11th September 1997, 700 years to the day that William Wallace defeated the English at the Battle of Stirling Bridge, Scotland went to the polls to vote on the issue of Devolution. On Saturday 13th, as part of European Heritage Day, along with other European cities, Aberdeen opened the doors of 25 places of architectural interest to its citizens. One of those buildings was the Mither Kirk of St Nicholas, which dates from the 12th century and houses the largest carillon (48 bells) in the British Isles.

Letter to a Dead Makar
(for Alistair Mackie, 1925-1995)

Your logic sharp's an axe that gleams and chops.
Your stanzas stir my thoughts
Like summer birch when the dark raven drops.

Hacking, hewing, honing, the rock face of cognition
You quarried words for hard linguistic nuggets
Your concepts, Vermeer-polished to precision

To your grave mooring, here is my poem to you.
Like Ulysses, your ship sailed far from view
To isles where Doric poetry seldom goes
Your craft, encrowned by thorns, bore forth a rose.
You set your shoulder to the wheel of Scots
But bogged and mired, it held a rutted road.
Its Muse, a muddied scarecrow in a field
A crippled haywain, crushed by the Past's load.

The Future lies, a bonnie, tumbled Venus,
And Scots draws back – emasculated penis!

A sickle, scything mediocrity
Such swathes you'd cut in spuriosity!
To most, Doric's a songbird in a cage
A tune, stuck in its throat
Circling and circling its small territory
Too coy, the macrocosm to engage.
You loosed its door. Encouraged it to soar
And raged, when it dropped down to hug the floor!

Sheaves of a changing country, Scots and Gael
Winnowed and weakened by the English flail,
In fresh-ploughed furrows, Gaelic's strewn around
Scots scatters careless seed, on stoney ground.

You were the goad that beat the Doric kye
Into a fertile zone
Now, they regroup and huddle, seeking the Safe, the Known,
Where Art's a shortbread tin.
Music's a kailyard drone.

The Three Graces: Embro Festival, 1995

Baldy professors ee them up an doon
(Spectacled grumphies, slivvrin ower each hoch)
Bare, as a scrapit soo frae dowp tae croon
Three bonnie quines. The trifle, in Art's troch.

The kirks are teem. The Gallery, is stappit
Thon bare-buff deems (cream puffs, wi cherries, tappit)
Staunin triumphant. Merble nymphies, nyakkit –
Flauntin, fit auld and creashie,
I keep happit.

The Dee, Oh

A keek o sun teets throw the wid
An fit wis happit, derkly hid
Gleams gowd, a liftit treisur lid
Alang the skinklin Dee, oh

A warm win showds the larick trees
Saft clouds o midgies skiff their eaves
The harebell dauncin ben the breeze
Wauchts sweet alang the Dee, oh

A yeitie wheeples, clear and wee
A willow reeshles like the sea
A mavis sails the lift, sae free
Sma piper ower the Dee, oh

The watter jibbles, amber, broon
The clashin wavelets chink a tune
A luver's sang, come liltin doon
The fragrant banks o Dee, oh

The puils birl roon like liquid braisse
Like fusky furlin in the glaiss
A dookin quine, wi heistit dress
Draws pleisur, frae the Dee, oh

The meenister extols the kirk
The fairmer, reezes oot the stirk
Gie me the glamourie o birk
The glimmerin waves o Dee, oh.

Out Vile Jelly!

Nasim Marie Jafry

It was as easy as going out to buy a loaf of bread: I left the flat, walked down the hill to the hospital, had my retinas zapped and came home.

Since the surgery I am constantly on the look-out for new symptoms. I wake up every morning expecting a shower of sparks and a curtain over the vision, a sure sign of retinal detachment. I drive Jeff crazy, lying in bed, squinting into the night, closing one eye, checking the other for flashes and floaters. He can sense my facial movements across the futon.

What are you doing?

Nothing . . . just checking.

Stop doing that eye thing . . . your eyes are fine. You just had them checked. Go to sleep.

I can't get the King Lear quote, *Out vile jelly! Where is thy lustre now?* out of my head. I go to bed with it and I wake up with it.

With bad things there's always a *before* and an *after.* Before the bad thing I was an ordinary myopic woman, doing my post-doc at UCLA. After the bad thing I was an ocular cripple.

I am the most short-sighted person I know and will put up with stabbing pains in my eyes rather than take my contacts out. I only wear my glasses in emergencies. They weigh me down, scaffolding round my head. The lenses are so thick my eyelashes bash against them and flatten.

I had gone for a routine eye-test. The optometrist told me that because I was so short-sighted, I was at risk of developing tears in my retinas. I gulped and he elaborated: the tears themselves were harmless, but left untreated they could become detachments which were much more serious. Then, they'd rush you to hospital and put sand-bags round your head to stop you from moving. Even with surgery there was no guarantee that your vision would be restored.

All news to me.

He dilated my eyes with drops and lo-and-behold found a well-sealed hole way at the back of my right eye. Nothing to worry about, he boasted, it's well-sealed.

I disagreed. I can worry about anything, and a well-sealed retinal hole was definitely something to worry about. I didn't trust this man. Anyway-he had fencing trophies in his office and irked me further by telling me that he was Scottish because his great-great-grandfather had been born in Aberdeen. Hey, you never know, maybe we're related, he said.

The pseudo-Scottish, fencing optometrist was none to friendly when I returned to his office with Jeff three hours later. He was just leaving. Full of tears, I told him I was extremely worried. He reassured me curtly that I had nothing to worry about and said he had to leave, that he was late for his fencing lesson.

For the next two weeks I tortured myself with the possibilities of a retinal detachment. I went to university book stores searching for ophthalmology texts. I bought a second-hand copy of *Illustrated Surgical Ophthalmology* and read and re-read the chapter on retinal detachments, scrutinising the colour photograph of the classic retinal tear which is shaped like a horse-shoe. I discovered that boxers and diabetic are also prone to retinal tears.

I was a wreck. My childhood dream came back where men in balaclavas are trying to get into the kitchen and I'm trying to lock the door and the key keeps slipping and turning in the lock. My childhood compulsion to check everything six times also came back. Six is my lucky number and as a child certain tasks had to be performed ritualistically every night. Before going to bed, I had to check that every electrical appliance was off by turning the switch at the socket off and on six times. And then I'd unplug it, so it didn't matter whether it was switched on or not. My sister suggested I put the kettle in the garden, just to be sure. Of course, the sockets in the States don't have switches, just two holes, but that didn't stop me. The front and back doors also had to be checked, especially on the way back from the toilet during the night. (That's the hardest time to resist).

Jeff was becoming drained by the nightly sessions of ocular psychotherapy and checking. He couldn't understand why I wouldn't make an appointment with an eye specialist if I was so worried. A few days later I chose an ophthalmologist from the Yellow Pages. His clinic was just down the hill, spitting distance from our flat.

I had to go or Jeff would have left me.

A few weeks later I was sitting in Dr Lazzeri's examination room.

– Dr Lazzeri will be with you shortly, his secretary announced cheerfully. I sat in the sinister black chair. I looked around at the charts and instruments and mirrors. The word ophthalmology clogged my throat like a wet dish-cloth.

The ophthalmologist came in. He was small with white hair and black glasses. He reminded me of Donahue, the cheesy talk show host.

– How are you today? What can I do for you?

When he talked his mouth didn't move much.

– I came for a second opinion. I saw an optometrist recently who said I have a retinal tear in my right eye. He says it's well-sealed, nothing to worry about.

My mouth was drying up with every word.

– I'm very short-sighted.

The doctor frowned and shook his head.

– There's no such thing as a well-sealed hole. These things don't heal. These optometrists don't know what they're talking about . . .

He was still shaking his head.

– Let's check your vision, then we'll look at the retinas.

I was beginning to hate that word. I wished he wouldn't say it. I took my contacts out.

– My goodness, you *are* near-sighted. Minus nine in both eyes! Okay
. . . these drops will dilate your pupils, and we can get a good look at the
retina. This will sting a little. You can go back to the waiting room now.

Retina, retina, retina! Was it the only word the man knew?

I sat in the waiting room in a myopic, dilated haze. I put my glasses on.
Two other patients, both elderly. I was probably his first patient under
seventy. One of them, a Chinese woman, had a bandage over her left eye.
Was her vile jelly intact?

Fifteen minutes later, the secretary shone a light in my eyes to check the
dilation.

– *Yup*, you're ready. She flashed me a smile and sent me back to the
black chair.

Enter Donahue.

– Okay, now just relax. He pressed a switch and the chair tilted back
ominously. He was standing above me with a miner's lamp on his head.
He examined the right eye first.

– Look up, all the way up. Look left, all the way left. I could see the
blood vessels of my eye. I heard him pick up an instrument.

– I'm just going to probe here gently. Scleral depression, that's what it's
called. I'd read the books. The fencing optometrist had also probed my
eye before announcing that I had a retinal hole.

– You've found something, haven't you?

He ignored my question and moved to the other side to examine the
left eye. More scleral depression. He finished and returned the chair to its
upright position.

– Have you had any flashers or floaters in either of your eyes?

– No . . . why?! What have you found?! Don't hide anything from me!
My heart was going to beat out of my chest.

– You have two small tears in your left eye and one small one in the
right. The good news is that they're tiny. The bad news is that because of
their position they could tear down. And with those *minus nine* eyes of
yours . . .

The rest of the conversation was in slow motion. He insisted on show-
ing me a plastic model of an eye to demonstrate the tears and and the risks
they posed. *If he were me he'd have the surgery to seal the tears. I had
insurance. Painless. No anaesthetic. No patch. Think about it.*

I was stunned. All I knew was that my retinas were torn and my legs
were stuck to the black chair with sweat. Thinking was out of the ques-
tion. It was up to him.

He smiled at me and told me not to worry and left me alone on the chair
with my new identity: a woman with torn retinas. The smiling secretary
(everyone was smiling) came in and asked for my insurance details. She
told me I was in great hands and scheduled me for laser treatment in two
days. She put more drops in my eyes to reverse the dilation and left me
alone again. I unstuck myself from the chair and gathered my things. I had

a strange urge to put the plastic model eye into my bag, but I didn't. I don't remember walking home.

I was inconsolable and couldn't stop crying. Usually my pessimism, which is my coping mechanism, prepares me for bad things, and when they happen, I'm not surprised. But not now. Nothing had prepared me for this. I was wrapped in grief and had Kafkaesque visions of lying in a darkened hospital room, sand-bags round my head, my retinas hanging on by a thread.

Jeff couldn't help. When he suggested that my anxiety was devouring me, I screamed at him, asking how he'd coped the last time he'd had laser surgery on his eyes. It could be worse, he said, trying to lighten things up, you could be a diabetic boxer.

The night before the surgery we watched a documentary about volcano rabbits. I didn't want it to end. I clung to Jeff on the sofa and tried to memorise every pore on his face. He told me that he loved me.

The awful morning dawned, unstoppable. By now I was exhausted and resigned to my fate. In two hours I was going to be blind, and that was that. I pretended I was in control of the decision *not* to go ahead with the surgery, but I knew I wasn't, not really. I had to go. We walked down the hill to the hospital. The sun was shining. I would never see it again. Jeff stayed outside to have a cigarette while I registered at the front desk.

The worst thing about any hospital procedure is the wrist-band they give you when you're admitted. Once you've got one, there's no going back, you're tagged, part of the hospital system. I signed the consent form and we went up to the Ophthalmology Department on the sixth floor. A nurse checked my vital signs and put drops in my eyes every fifteen minutes until my irises had all but disappeared. I held Jeff's hand in a vice.

Cue Donahue. I was hoping he'd forgotten. You might as well buy the guide dog now, I said to Jeff, before going into the treatment room.

I was worried that there would be an earthquake during the surgery and Donahue'd zap the wrong part of my eye.

– What if there's an earthquake?

– Don't worry. It'll be a piece of cake. Dr Lazzeri smiled benignly.

– What if I blink? I stalled him with another question.

– You won't be able to blink. He put some anaesthetising drops in my eyes and switched off the light. As good as his word, he put something on my left eye to prevent me from blinking and told me it was essential that I keep still. I lay on the hospital trolley, rigid.

The argon laser descended on me. *Zap, zap, zap!* Scooshes of water between the green zaps to cool the cornea down. *Zap, zap, zap!* Each zap lasted a twentieth of a second. It was like being on Star Trek. In five minutes he'd finished the first eye. I sat up. I couldn't see anything out of my left eye. Blind panic.

– I can't see! It's all black! Everything's black!

Donahue patted me on the shoulder. – Don't worry. You've had a very bright light in your eye. It's just the after-effect. It won't last. I should have warned you.

No shit, Sherlock.

Gradually the blackness faded to crimson, then a greyish purple.

– Can I do the other eye now?

Five minutes later he'd finished. I had survived the laser coagulation! Before leaving the treatment room he told me to take it easy and not to wear my contacts for a few days. I heard him cheerfully tell Jeff, who was outside waiting like an expectant father, that I was fine and just resting for a few minutes. I sat there, feeling strangely elated in my greyish purple daze.

I left the hospital boasting to Jeff that I had just had laser surgery. I was quite proud of myself. I remember going back to the flat and switching on the radio. A gunman had taken a guy hostage in a downtown bank. Everything was the same, nothing had changed. I just happened to have had my torn retinas sealed with an argon laser.

For the next three weeks I had the constant feeling that I had just been blinded by a camera-flash. Colours seemed washed out, black text looked grey. I had to wear sun-glasses even when I was indoors. I cried a lot and continued to refer to my ophthalmology manual for support. Until Jeff hid it. It's bad for you, he said. It's just feeding your neuroses. I pleaded with him, but he stuck to his guns. You're not having it back, he admonished. It's damaging you. It's damaging *us*. The us part frightened me more than not having the book so I shut my mouth.

I'd educated the people at work who now knew as much as me about retinal tears. They too had become accustomed to my squinting and covering one eye in my grand quest for symptoms. If you've got spots or floaters they show up best in a white room. The source of this gem of information was Vikram, whom I share an office with. Vikram's uncle had had floaters all his life. He had a detachment when he was sixty. (I imagine a small, thin man in Bombay, sandbagged and terrified.) Our office walls are unremittingly white, an ideal background for the checker.

A month after the surgery I went back to Dr Lazzeri for a check-up. He seemed tired. It was the first time I'd seen him as a person, as someone who could get tired and not just as a firer of laser beams. He did the usual things: dilation, probing, and scleral depression. Everything's just dandy, he said, as the chair tilted upright again. But, remember, the first signs of spots or floaters or flashers, you come straight to me. Those eyes have to last you a long time. Thanks, I said, eternally grateful.

A year's passed since the bad thing and I continue to torture myself with retinal possibilities. I can see that fucking hospital from my kitchen window, beckoning me every day to take part in its sinister laser game-show, *Come on down! Get those retinas sealed!*

When it all gets too much, I go and see Dr Lazzeri. He reassures me every time, but I still can't get the kitchen door locked.

Louise

Valerie Thornton

When I got home, it was only Dad that was there.

"She's visiting Louise," he said, leading me into the kitchenette.

I was surprised, and pleased too, because my mother and I don't get on too well. Nothing definite, just a kind of wariness.

Ever since Louise died, when I was fourteen and she was eleven, my mother has celebrated a series of gloomy anniversaries throughout the year. Louise's birthday, of course, her death day, her funeral day and the anniversary of the date when the reason for her listlessness and fainting fits was confirmed.

Dad fills the kettle through the red rubber spout on the cold tap that lets you direct the water to different parts of the sink. It always seems to be perished.

He makes coffee with carnation milk because that way it reminds him of the coffee they had in Paris, my mother and him, on their honeymoon. A splash of romance and hope and happy memories from the red and white tin whose triangular opening will congeal to translucent cream lumps in the fridge.

Today is the sixth. As usual, I'd forgotten. It would have been, it is, Louise's twenty first birthday.

Dad lays out the cups and saucers on the tray. Fading yellow roses on the fluted china, with a fragmenting gold line piped around the edges and the rise of the knobbly handle. This is the only place I ever drink coffee from a cup. I live in flat-land, mug-land, and always take it black now.

"Derek's coming over too," he says, as we sit down in the living room. I don't sit in my mother's chair, but in one of the ones for visitors.

It's always strange for me going back to visit my parents. It's home, but not home. Ringing the bell feels alien, when for years I tumbled noisily in the door and to a cry of "Who's there?" yelled triumphantly "Me!" and waited for Mum to guess, usually wrongly, whether it was me or Louise.

But not ringing is no longer appropriate.

"She's very proud of you, you know," Dad says. "But she'll never let on to you. You know what she's like."

We look at each other. We know.

Derek arrives and Dad goes through to make a third cup of coffee.

"I see you got a good review in the *Courier*. Well done, kid!" Derek beams at me. "You should get one for over the mantelpiece, Dad!" he calls. "She's very collectable now, our Kate."

"I know! They're lovely paintings, though I say so myself. I popped in last week."

"Has Mum been down yet?" Derek asks me quietly.

"I don't think so. She hasn't said anyway."

Derek plonks himself down in my mother's seat and stretches his legs out in front of the electric fire. "Aye, she's a funny woman," he says, looking at her painting of Loch Lomond from Balloch above the fireplace. "You can see where you get it from, though."

"Derek – did you remember – today?"

"Today?"

"Louise."

"Not another anniversary! What's it this time – the cutting of the first tooth day?"

"Derek – stop it! She'll be back in a minute. Louise would have been twenty-one today."

Derek reflects for a moment. "Well, she's not, is she?"

Dad brings the coffee into the silence. "Now, now be gentle, Derek. She still hurts."

"So do we all, but life goes on."

My mother's key turns in the lock and we start, guilty.

"But **you're** doing well, aren't you, Derek?" I say brightly. Too brightly, into the gap between the door opening and the door closing.

"Hello, dear!" Dad calls and my mother comes into the room, beige raincoat, grey hair and brown shopping bag.

"Hello, you two – how nice to see you here. I just nipped out for some cakes from MacPhersons. I know you like their empire biscuits," she says, smiling at Derek, bright-eyed.

"Mum! I'm on a diet!"

"Nonsense!" she says, backing away. "You're celebrating! Isn't he a clever lad?" and she looks at me, wide-eyed.

Derek has been promoted to Assistant Sales Manager. He sells washing machines and fridges and dishwashers and tumble driers – white metal boxes to make living easier. He is three years older than me, and cheerful.

"Yes, it's great!" I say, meaning it. "He's worked hard for it and it's nice they've recognised that."

"I was telling Mrs Murphy next door about it and she says to pass on her congratulations too." My mother beams, basking in the reflected glory of Derek's success.

"But what about Kate? She's got a lovely collection together – have you been to the gallery yet?"

"Em . . . not yet," my mother says, suddenly distant. "I'll just go and get the tea on."

It's alright. I'm used to it.

At first everything was lovely, years ago, and me and Louise would sit round the kitchen table with Mum and she'd teach us to draw and paint. Louise was always better than me, even though she was younger, and her drawings went on the wall much more often than mine.

"You take after me," Mum would say to her, smiling across me. "One day you'll maybe get to Art School and become a real painter."

My mother would have loved to have done that. But, as she says dismissively, she never had the training. And she won't go to classes now because she says it's too late.

But Louise grew pale and thin and tired and too weak to hold a pencil. I would do drawings for her and take them into the hospital. Then when they let her home again, I'd sit by her bed and draw outside things for her. Flowers and streets and houses and shops and places where she knew, where we all knew, she wouldn't go again. It seemed like she was dying forever.

And now it seems like she's been dead forever. But we don't talk about it.

There's this lovely smell coming from the kitchen, an old smell of mince and onions. No garlic or fancy spices. And there will be doughballs too.

My mother bustles in and pulls out the table and puts up the leaf. A movement as old as the marriage and as familiar.

She deals out the places from a fistful of shiny cutlery and goes into the kitchenette again. And I notice then that there are five places.

"Derek!" I hiss. "She's set a place for Louise."

"Christ!" he says, as Dad rises to collect our cups.

I hear my mother busy stirring in the kitchen, beating the flour and water for the doughballs in the white china bowl, and I rise to go to the table.

I pick up one place setting, the extra one on my side of the table, where Louise and I used to sit together, and I begin to slide my cutlery over to take up a centre place, when my mother walks in.

"What are you doing?" she asks, as if she were asking if it were raining. Then she realises.

"Don't!" she screeches at me. And she rushed up to me, knocks the cutlery from my hand and hits me, hard, on the face, then, sobbing, she falls to the floor scrabbling for the cutlery with fumbling fingers. "That's Louise's place. You can't take it away! My baby's twenty-one!"

Derek is still, Dad is frozen, coffee cups in hand, and I am scared. There is a feeling of storm in the air, of lightning about to split us apart with blinding brightness.

"Louise is dead, Mum."

Her back heaves and a shuddering howl breaks out. I cannot touch this woman, whose child I am. I cannot comfort her. I am a living reminder of her loss. Of her losses. Of her pain.

And the flash of lightning, this storm which has been gathering for ten years, flares bright among us with the certainty of truth.

I see now where I went wrong. I should never have realised my mother's dream, not for herself, but for Louise, who would have been the greatest artist. Whose talent was struck down. Thwarted. Her paintings would have touched the soul.

And I realise now, in this chilling moment, that if Louise had lived and I had died, I would not have been mourned like this.

And I become angry.

"Louise is dead! Gone! She died ten years ago. Let her go! You never have!"

"Kate . . . " my Dad is saying, and he has his hand on my arm. I cannot remember the last time he touched me. "Katy, enough."

"No, it's not! She's never forgiven me!"

"Forgiven you?"

"For not dying instead of Louise. **She** should have been here today, not me, **she** should have been here all these days and not me."

"Katy, we both love you more than we can say."

I know that he loves me, that when I was little, when I was his only daughter, he worshipped me. And in that moment, I know too my mother's jealousy. That my father loved me in a deeper, purer, more powerful way than he could ever love this woman who is my mother.

But that had all changed with Louise.

"**She** doesn't love me."

And I watch my mother gathering herself, rising from the floor, her knuckles white around Louise's cutlery. I see as clearly as I see the bones, why everything I've ever done was wrong. Why my gold medal at Art School was never mentioned, why she never comes to see my work, why she finds pain in every brush-stroke I make, every breath I draw.

The shutters have come down again. Her eyes are veiled. And the smell of mince and doughballs fills the room with a homely warmth.

Dad holds out his hand to her and she gives him the cutlery. He puts it in the drawer and she drifts into the kitchenette. Dad sits down again, and Derek, who hasn't moved, turns the watch on his wrist around and around and around.

I sit on the visitor's chair again and we all wait, quietly. I am shaking and very, very cold. I don't think I'll be able to eat. I'm supposed to be dead. I'm supposed to be the one in the silver frame, on top of the television.

Louise watches us from pride of place, smiling all the way from primary seven.

Everything is back to normal.

I breathe deeply and try to relax.

My mother is dishing up the meal. "Dinner's ready," she calls in a clear steady voice.

I draw comfort from the sound of her composure.

We take our places at the table and she lays the food before us, her own plate, with slightly less than anyone else's, last.

"This looks nice," Derek says, but his voice is more shrill than normal.

"Well, just begin," my mother says, and I feel the storm is blowing over. That in the calm we may begin to talk, and understand, and maybe we can draw closer and break this barren pattern of empty words and silence.

Maybe my mother thinks the same, I don't know, but she smiles at me. Gently.

"We'll just begin," she says. "I've put Louise's in the oven, she'll be back from Brownies soon."

And we pick up our knives and forks, and begin to eat, the way we always do. The way we always will.

Stanley Trevor

Graffiti

*"Lady Jane Grey, Foxe reports, when denied
pen and ink in the Tower, managed to scratch
out a poem with a pin."*

J W Saunders, The Profession of English Letters

1

mind crumbles
like rockfall

the insistent hum
and drum of traffic
rumbles and roars
like a discontented sea
the shoreland poisoned
weed-patched raw dirt
littered with debris

a rabble of gulls
wheel and deal
and scream for garbage

headlights turned on
hasten the departing sun

after dark
there are no lamps

winter bites
deep as decay

> *Deirdre Mackay is a fat slag and
> will shag anything that dangles*

in this corner
time has stopped

2

a curve of rock locked land
to the highlands and islands

bare ruined stone

skulls of history

sightless windows
filter yesterday

weather-broken

the language
of dispossession

the fate of those
whose names
are writ in glass

> *Glencalvie people*
> *the wicked generation*[1]

death pours
from their concave sockets

3

winter cleanses the river

pine trees
transposed for graveyards
tire of ice and bone
of wet wind weather

ivy clings
to lifeless trunks
the illusion of life

branches break
weary of too much strength

on the slatted bench
I know that I know
that passers-by
overcoated
to an other world
will pass me by

"a solitary mister"

> *gifted by the family*
> *in loving memory* . . .

between the poems
your image lies
like a broken bowl

---

1. A reference to the church at Croick. When the last 18 families in Glencalvie were evicted during the Clearances, they took refuge in the churchyard, some 90 souls including children as young as 7, where they slept under nothing but a tarpaulin with only straw and rushes to protect them. They were not permitted to seek shelter in the church itself as this would be 'sacrilegious'. Their names and plight were recorded in messages scratched on the east window of the church including the above quote, having been persuaded that their fate was punishment for their sins.

Fish Fingers and the Silver Fish: An Appreciation of George Byatt

George Gunn

There are those who are before their time and whose innovative work and vision is never appreciated by the society and culture which gave them birth. Then there are others who shoot to prominence almost at the outset of their careers, but fade like the bloom of a flower. George Byatt, the playwright who died so tragically in November 1996 was definitely of the former when you think of the Scottish theatre and strangely enough was of the latter in the world of the BBC and television generally. This is typical of George Byatt. But it is of the playwright about whom I wish to write.

I first met George in 1982 when his theatre company PKF, The Peace Keeping Force, were touring with *The Brus*, a play about the Scottish Wars of Independence of the fourteenth century, and which I think is George's masterpiece. That play and George Byatt changed my life. I had the privilege of working very closely with him in the mid-eighties, for roughly four years. In that time I learned so much about the theatre, and whatever success I subsequently had, and all the work I've done since then, are due to my education from and with George Byatt and Theatre PKF.

In 1982 I was no playwright. Some may argue I'm still not, but that's another thing. When I met George I realised I'd seen him before. It was at the Traverse in 1978. Then I was drilling for oil in the North Sea, but that period was coming to an end and I was searching for something else. I'd always been curious about the theatre. I went to the Traverse in Edinburgh on my two weeks off. My uncle George More was a former members and I was going to see a play called *Kong Lives* with my friend, the actor Hugh Loughlan. Anyway, we were in the foyer just about to go into the bar, the theatre was upstairs. Suddenly two men came rolling down the stairs wrapped around each other. One was George Byatt, the author of *Kong Lives*. The other was the designer. They were having what George told me later was a "creative discussion problem": George wanted a kitchen sink put on a beer crate. The play was set in a Glasgow back to back and was, George informed me, an "anti-kitchen sink play". The designer said he had his reputation to think of and couldn't possibly have a kitchen sink presented like that on his wonderful set. So they were arguing about this at the top of the stairs, had lost their balance and, as they say, came a-tumbling down. George also said later that *Kong Lives* was originally called *How Gracie Fields Betrayed the Working Class*. But the Traverse didn't like that either. So much for the innovation of the *avant garde*.

Above all George was an innovator. He was of the opinion that when the playwright wrote a play it was like a beautiful silver fish and when the theatre got around to putting it on what the people got was fish fingers. He just saw the world from a completely different point of view from anyone else. I had done nothing in my life. Sure I had published a few poems

Photographs provided by Lucy Byatt
Painting by Kara Wilson

but I had never written a play and knew practically nothing about the theatre. George changed all that. Because of him I wrote my first play *Roughneck* which was performed at the Traverse, ironically, in 1984.

George always described himself as an anarchist. He believed in the deconstruction of power and in the power of the imagination to change people's perceptions. He believed in the ability of the individual within a collective and cooperative society to achieve and enjoy freedom. He was a liberationist in the true sense and tried to bring all this and more to his theatre. Sometimes he didn't succeed. Sometimes he could be thrawn, cantankerous and downright perverse. With actors, however he was usually generous, loyal. Because he didn't believe in directors, he always encouraged actors to find the creative base of their performance from within themselves. Too much of our theatre is a power relationship between director and actor. Actors basically have to do what the director tells, or asks, them to do. George wanted to liberate the actor, the writer and the audience.

His theory of the internalising and externalising of how theatre works I found, over time, to be completely true. Basically it went like this: the writer goes amongst their own people and internalises the story of the society they live in. The writer then externalises this experience by writing a play. The actor internalises the play and in performance externalises it through the production. The audience, for their part, internalise the performance experience and when they leave the theatre they go back into their society, they externalise yet again by talking to their family and friends. Then along comes the writer again. And so it goes on.

This internalisation and externalisation circle – one of George's favourite shapes, is exactly how theatre works in my experience. It is the dynamic which gives theatre its power. It has sustained theatre-making over the many centuries from the first time the tribe gathered to sing their collective song. According to Lope de Vega, theatre is at society's core: "The passionate combat of two human beings on a platform". George believed in passionate combat, in human beings and loved a platform. Morris Blythman the Glasgow songwriter wrote, and I paraphrase, "The writer should be with the people, for the people, in their struggle – right or wrong."

That is the tradition George, the writer, came from: that radical tradition of West Coast literature which more or less began in the 18th century, of which Robert Burns was an important component, through to Tannahill and the weaver poets of such places as Paisley, through to Hugh Mac-Diarmid and right up to the present day. Morris Blythman knew George very well and there was no doubt that he influenced George's work from the late seventies onwards. Morris's songs such as the 'anti-polaris Ding Dong Dollar' and the 'Scottish Break Away' actually laid the foundation for plays such as, most importantly, *The Clyde is Red* and others such as *Why Does the Pope Not Come to Glasgow*. I think it was Morris Blythman's mixture of socialism, republicanism and nationalism that formed many of George's later ideas about Scotland's future, culturally and politically.

These ultimately found their fusion in *The Brus*. For here was a play which addressed the ideas of freedom, nationality, independence and culture head on. From Barbour's *Brus* of the 15th century George put the maxim "For freedom is a noble thing which no man gives up but with his life" in a new way. George grew to be wholly committed to the idea of an independent Scottish Socialist Republic. That was his dream, and it has become my dream too. To paraphrase the American novelist Carson McCullers, "If you have no place to come from, you have no place to go". George saw clearly that by suppressing, however subtly and in whatever form, a people's culture, you suppress their ability to have confidence in themselves and their identity and therefore you can control them.

There is no doubt, because I spoke to him about it often, that he felt neglected but he would never admit it in public. After the Traverse days in the 70s no theatre company would touch a George Byatt play with a ten foot tarry pole. Admittedly, George stuck rigidly to his principles and would not bend one inch. *The Clyde is Red* had to be read script in hand; Robert Bruce had to be played by a woman; all those things I'm sure didn't help. But that's what he believed and that's what he wanted, and he was prepared to pay the heavy price for it. So he was ignored by mainstream Scottish theatre. George simply went underground. He formed Theatre PKF; he helped set up The Edinburgh Playwrights Workshop. The influence of PKF hasn't yet come through. It will, but there is no doubting the lasting influence of Edinburgh Playwrights Workshop. There writers such as myself, Rona Munro, John Clifford, Peter Arnott and many more, were first seen and heard, all selflessly helped and encouraged by George when he knew inside that for him while he was alive the show was more or less over. The Playwrights Workshop gave writers the confidence and support to write. All the writers I mentioned have gone on to win awards and gain great acclaim. All benefited from knowing and working with George Byatt.

And perhaps here is the ultimate, tragic irony: now that he is safely dead, Scottish theatres may begin to give mainstage productions of *The Brus*. Perhaps we can look forward to seeing it at the Assembly Hall at the Edinburgh Festival? Perhaps it will be compared to David Lyndsay's *Ane Satire of the Three Estates* as a work of genius, and join the canon of Scottish theatre classics. Perhaps *The Brus* will tour the world and George Byatt will be as famous a name as Bertold Brecht and Sean O'Casey? Perhaps. It would take some time. It should happen, and if it does I know George will be smiling down from whatever celestial circle workshop discussion about how to democratise the angels he's conducting and he'll laugh a little laugh to himself, but I know that he would be glad and proud and so he should be. I miss my old comrade and I can't believe he's dead. For to misquote Burns as is appropriate "To know him was to love him". But thankfully through his work, that most remarkable of men, George Byatt, lives on.

Note: George Byatt's article, 'Fish Fingers or The Predicament of the Scottish Playwright', in *Chapman* 35-6: *The State of Scotland –A Predicament for the Scottish Writer?* is still available £5.00.

Billy Watt

Greek Muffs

Medusa in Clyde Square

dji heer aboot it
seems she'd been steyin
in this sorta convint

when sum heed bummer
sea captn ur sumhm
goes an rayps ur

nixt thing his wife fines oot
maims the lassie fur life
fayss wurss than the backia buss

diz nuthinty him but
aw naw
seems she wis a fine-lookin lassie befoar

naebdi wid lookit ur
twice efter that
then ti croon it aw

this this sykopath
goes an slits ur throat
they found ur lyin

wi a bottla White Horss
under the crayns
o Kincaids yerd

depressn intit
furst the gaffer rooins yi
then yir ain kind finish the job

Achilles: Mean, Moody . . . And Reticent

clank clank
amma tank

gizyur best
oan ma chist

canny feel
septma heel

20 heroes
deedna day

stript thur ermir
hit the hay

in ma tent
in the huff

coodny thoal it
hud inuff

lost ma mayt
inna fire

thats ma stoary
gun fur hire

Nae Manacles On Heracles

– gitnyur feet aw manky
inna staybl
disny mayk yi a horss
Ah telt im

– giz naynyir hoamspun lip
siz he
waggin that broth pot heed
that lyins mayn onnum

see me hen
goany be a star
see me
an alimpick champyin

– ivry Friday night the saym
nuckls rid raw
blid doonies shurt
fayss hingin affum

the *Hydra*
the *RAF club*
they aw yooz im
fur thur ain ends

but Ahl tell yi
if he cums in the night
hawf cut
nae shurt onnies back

hees fur a roastin

Cassandra

throo ma vayns
throo ma hart
throo ma marra

the greetna wayns
dumpt in plastic bags
ur burnt wi fags
ur strapt inti boams

throo ma vayns
throo ma hart
throo ma marra

ull foak mugdin the gutr
granny deednur flat
raypt wummin n kids
the torcht
the torchurd
an wurss
so wurss Ah canny say it

Ah try ti tell thum
fi ma vayns
an ma hart
an ma marra

but thull naw lissn
they slag me
playg me
tell me ti piss aff

light nup they say
light nup Sandra
but Ah say
the nayms naw Sandra
its *Cass*andra

Furst Fitn Tantalus

jist look at im
fayss sukt in
like a goats erss   *I will drink*

wawtch im noo
ivry time
he gets a hawf

he goes inti the kitchn
then emptiz it
inti a sawsur   *I will drink no more*

so whinny offurs hawfs
tae furst fitturs
they doant know

hees poarn thur whisky
oot thi sawsur
inti thur glesses   *of the fruit*

so
thur aw drinkn
thur ain whisky

an aw the time
yir man heers boatl
huzny been oapnd   *of the fruit of the vine*

Echo On Narcissus

the day he saw a mirrur   *mirrur*
– that wis the end

Ah got anarexic
widny go oot

lost fur wurds   *wurds*
jist repeetn him aw the time

eez ay sekshul Ah think   *ink*
nuhn but a wangkur

trip owriz toes
fur looknit umself inna pudl   *pudl*

n yit
n yit

whut a ride
a holy ride

Eros

therrs this wee thing
this wee partikl
the weeist partikl
thurriz

so wee that naebdiz
ever found wan
its cauld the GRAVITON
n yit

by the grayss o gravity
n aw ma arras
its whit hauds us aw
thegither

Orpheus

jist doant think dae yi
we wir ingaged n aw
she wisnae jist a groopie ken

so wir boamin doon the A71
in this saft tap wiv wired
jist fur the buzzie it

hur n the bayss playr
wurrin the back seat
gigglin n messna roon ken

shooda trustid ur mair
but Ah hudti look back
hudti see whit they wir upti

n it wis ded dark
ded hard ti see thum
so Ah hud ti turn right roon ken

next thing therrs this big artic
apeerd fi naewherr
right inti the backie it

Ah mind the screemin
n the flashn lightsie the pigs
didny huv thur seatbelts oan ken

noo thur oot ti get me
aw ur relayshins
Ahm deed yi ken

ma contracts oot

Reviews

Lives Out On The Borderlands

A History of Scottish Women's Writing, ed Douglas Gifford and Dorothy McMillan, EUP, £19.95.

In 'Listening to the Women Talk', published in 1993 in *The Scottish Novel since the Seventies*, an eloquent contributor to the volume discussed here, Carol Anderson, wrote:

> There is a strong case for arguing that there is a women's tradition in our literature, not entirely separate from writing by men, but with its own qualities, and unduly neglected. This tradition should be highlighted and considered in its own right, as well as integrated into the more general view of our traditions.

Since the early 90s especially, pressure (see 'The Women's Forum', *Chapman* 74-75, 76, 77) has increased on the Scottish academic establishment to review the tacit assumptions by which the "'Scottish Tradition in Literature' has been both male generated and male fixated" (Gifford/McMillan). The introduction, 43 chapters and extensive bibliography of *A History of Scottish Women's Writing* constitute a scholarly but accessible attempt to produce a redressive vision of Scottish women's writing that goes beyond homogenous, 'herstory'-style separatism. Instead it locates the critical moments and complexities in a story of writing and mind in which women's "double-voiced discourse" has sought to "imitate or revise the tropes of the male tradition" (Elaine Showalter, 1993).

Overdue as it is, the intervention undertaken by this volume has not come too late to engage with the "absence of a clearly visible female literary tradition" (Gifford/McMillan). One delight of this book is that its revelations and valorisations send one hurrying away from almost every chapter to interrogate the authority and standards of Academy and Canon, only to find with its editors that a truly balanced projection of Scottish literature, incorporating the largely unmapped terrain of women's writing, has yet to be written.

The timely arrival of this publication can be easily demonstrated by collating its findings with those of three recent, influential international perspectives on Scottish literature, one of which is mentioned in the introduction: in *The Norton Anthology of Literature by Women* (1996), according to Gifford and McMillan, "nothing from Scottish literature, not even one short story from Mrs Oliphant, finds a place". Secondly, a fairly spacious (8 columns) 'Scottish Poetry' entry in the *New Princeton Encyclopedia of Poetry and Poetics* (1993) mentions nine women. This might at first seem hopeful until it is noted that five of these (Jean Elliot, Lady Nairne, Violet Jacob, Marion Angus and Helen Cruickshank) occur in one short sentence remarking that their "literary songs" "tend toward sentimentalism", two others (Sheena Blackhall and Valerie Gillies) are listed in the final sentence, while the remaining two, Liz Lochhead and Tessa Ransford, are mentioned in passing as examples of "unapologetically" expressed "feminism" and "feminist rage" respectively.

Finally, and closer to home, the two published volumes (covering c. 1350 to c. 1900 – a third is projected) of John McCordick's gigantic anthology *Scottish Literature* contain fewer than 120 pages (of 2,460!) devoted to women's writing. Figures as bleak as these suggest that this book provides a powerful incitement to reverse the *status quo*, while itself contributing to the process.

Robert Crawford prefaces his contribution 'Burns's Sister', with an "emblematic" incident on 17 November 1862 in which the path of aspiring medical student Elizabeth Garrett, on her way to a chemistry lecture at St Andrew's University, was blocked by the novelist Susan Ferrier's nephew Professor James Frederick Ferrier, who invented the word 'epistemology': he "stood in the doorway and asked Miss Garrett to turn back. She did." What Crawford does not mention is that the debarred Elizabeth Garrett, following a circuitous, untrodden route devised as much by herself as by the hostile medical establish-

88

ment, went on to climb to the top of her profession. She become not only a mother to three children, but the first woman to gain the right in England to practice as a surgeon, first woman member of the BMA, first woman Dean of a medical school and, indeed, Britain's first woman mayor.

Crawford's argument is that feminist historiography "must be something more than the simple search for emblematic precursors of modern feminism", but the facts should nonetheless interest us. Literary history will be blind if the maps it evolves cannot account for the winding 'back roads', private diversions and cross-country hikes sought by women whose access to public routes taken by their male colleagues was blocked, out of "regard" (Crawford) for the propriety of gender roles.

In her reassessment of Violet Jacob, Carol Anderson writes that Jacob

> still has not found a secure place on the literary maps. Much of her work deals with areas and subjects far from the centres of power; she examines lives 'out on the borderlands, lives for which the central interpretative devices of culture don't quite work'.

Or in Moira Burgess's chapter on 'The modern Historical Tradition' (focusing on Jane Oliver, Naomi Mitchison, Dorothy Dunnett and Sian Hayton), Mitchison, a young mother in the twenties, famously passes down one such back road with a "big notebook . . . opened out at my end of the pram so that I could write my book while I went on slowly pushing". There is a small irony (underlining the editors' awareness that their 'history' will be deceptive if it attempts a "smooth story of sisterhood") that it is precisely to Naomi Mitchison that we owe an assessment of Elizabeth Garrett "by the standards of the 1920s", concluding "that she was neither a brilliant nor a born doctor".

Whether taking a view of most individual eminent women writers or writing under more generalised headings – e.g. 'Viragos of the Periodical Press', 'Women and Nation', two chapters on 'Twentieth Century Poetry' or three on 'Contemporary Fiction', etc. – the

40 authors of this volume offer "possible maps of the country and a series of possible routes through it". They also show how privacy, invisibility, anonymity, asylum and exile, whether enforced or preferred, have been known by Scottish women writers for centuries and have sometimes been exploited in strategies which have enabled writers to overcome marginalisation by the male tradition. However, in a chapter on 'Non-fiction Writing in the Eighteenth and Early Nineteenth Centuries', McMillan warns that

> it has become a cliché of the investigation of private writing . . . that we look . . . for evidence of an explicit or covert process of self-construction, a kind of compensation of public powerlessness.

Two chapters suggest that the search for self-constructions of the individual psyche would be particularly unrewarding in the field of Gaelic writing. Indeed the word 'writer', as Meg Bateman points out in 'Women's Writing in Scottish Gaelic since 1750', is itself a "misnomer", and even the work of Màiri Mhòr was "produced without recourse to writing." Almost by definition, "oral work is not individualistic". The literary or sub-literary work of many women was "a service to the community rather than to the Muse". This did not preclude conflict with a male bardic tradition, however. Màiri nighean Alasdair Ruaidh recalled in Anne Frater's opening chapter on 'The Gaelic Tradition up to 1750', is reputed to have been exiled by the MacLeods of Dunvegan to punish her boldness in competing with the bards. This was evidently ineffective, for she is thought to have composed more poetry after her expulsion than before it.

Sarah M Dunnigan's immensely readable chapter on 'Scottish Woman Writers c. 1560-c.1650' shows how Christian Lindsay's sole extant work, the sonnet 'Oft haive I hard, bot ofter fund it treu', implies the "'invisibility', or irrelevance, of her gender" to the extent that she adopts a "masculinist . . . rhetoric of intimacy". Mary Stuart, by contrast, has left a surprisingly large poetic *corpus*, allowing readers to construe her "intellectual and spiritual biography" from her own words, counterbalancing the iconising distortions inflicted upon her as 'Mary, Queen of Scots'. Lines by Mary Oxlie –

From an untroubled mind should Verses flow;
My discontents makes mine too muddy show;
And hoarse encumbrances of household care
Where these remaine, the muses ne're repaire

– anticipate, across the centuries, Peter Butter's resumée in the closing words of his sensitive chapter on Elizabeth Grant: "The keen eye and the quick intelligence endured, but the needs of the practical present blunted the imagination", or Margaret Oliphant's despairing cry (cited by Merryn Williams):

How I have been handicapped in life! Should I have done better if I had been kept, like her [George Eliot], in a mental greenhouse and taken care of?

Mary Ellen Brown and Kirsteen McCue, in their chapters on balladry and song, show how women may have been the anonymous chief-preservers, performers and consumers of ballad-poetry, making it frequently impossible to trace the authorship of a song, as in the case of the beautiful 'Ca' the Yowes to the Knowes', which may originally be attributable to Isobel Pagan (1741-1821) rather than Burns. While Burns (as a man) or Pagan (as the keeper of a "kind of low tippling house") could compose and perform their songs with relative impunity, this freedom was not felt by Carolina Oliphant, Lady Nairne, who, under the pseudonym of Mrs Bogan of Bogan, wrote a great number of popular and Jacobite songs (including 'Charlie is my Darling' and 'Will Ye No Come Back Again'). Her husband is reported to have "remained ignorant to his dying day that his wife had been guilty of song-writing", and there are accounts of her "mysterious visits to Purdie the publisher clad as a Scottish gentlewoman of the olden time".

A fascinating chapter by Amanda Gilroy shows how the poet and playwright Joanna Baillie "negotiates the boundaries of the space allotted to femininity in the first half of the nineteenth century". In the uneasy tension between fame and femininity, the public

act of representation threatens to undermine gender and class identity by making a spectacle of the writer, and figuratively forging links between poetesses and prostitutes, both of whom display their wares in a marketplace ordered by men. The question, then, is how to negotiate the crossing from private to public, to write within the geography of the feminine.

Gilroy argues that Baillie's exemplary public poetic status "depends on the perception of her unviolated privacy". As a strategy, this is not merely restrictive: "Baillie's 'womanly' behaviour means that she resists being appropriated as the object of the gaze and being written into a (foreign) script that she cannot control." At the same time, Baillie's texts are "complicit with the intertwined ideologies of gender and imperialism".

In that she sees how women's poetry can be overwhelmed and constrained by the (unwanted) embrace of the establishment, there is an unexpected parallel between Dorothy McMillan's discussion of contemporary poetry and Gilroy's analysis of Baillie. According to McMillan "the main problem facing women writers today may be the curse of acceptance rather than neglect." Critics, she notices, are "too willing to read women's writing as having as its sole aim the speaking back of marginalised or even colonised female voices". Instead, McMillan's chapter shows that contemporary women, while reclaiming lost ground, often move on "to the planting of crops far more exotic and various than are covered by the simple formula of women's experience". McMillan's fluid non-essentialism is echoed in Gifford's ('Contemporary Fiction 1: Tradition and Continuity'), discovering – among other things –

a new recognition of gender inclusiveness in which traditional barriers between male and female writing in Scotland are beginning to crumble as increasingly female and male writers avoid specific gender identification in their work, so that a new fiction emerges in which men write women, and women write men.

It is impossible to do justice to the great work of revelation and recovery contained in this *History*, except to say that any history or anthology of Scottish literature in the foreseeable future will inevitably be judged by its standards.

Iain Galbraith

Leabhraichean Gàidhlig

Bogha-frois san Oidhche/ Rainbow in the Night, Fearghas MacFhionnlaigh, The Handsel Press, £9.95; *Ainmeil an Eachdraidh*, ed Ruaraidh MacThomais, Gairm, £7.50; *Chì Mi: Bàrdachd Dhòmhnaill Iain Dhonnchaidh/* I See: The Poetry of Donald John MacDonald, ed and transl Bill Innes, Birlinn, £12.99.

It is a healthy sign that three recent and diverse Gaelic publications (one offering no English translation) should appear, courtesy of three different publishers. Two of these books offer non-Gaels a taste of 20th century Gaelic poetry's curious interplay between the traditional and the modern, while the other, essays about people 'Famous in History', is a worthy addition to the bookshelves of Gaelic learners and native speakers alike.

Fearghas MacFhionnlaigh's poetry, which I first saw anthologised in *An Aghaidh na Siorruidheachd/* In the Face of Eternity, struck me as exceptional in its inventiveness and its manipulation of Gaelic, which, under his pen, becomes a thoroughly modern, almost futuristic, language. MacFhionnlaigh is an art teacher (he designed the bookjacket) and a devout Calvinist Christian (his faith gives the book much of its emotional charge). In 1990, Ciaran, the poet's son, was struck by a brain virus. As he lay paralysed in hospital (in the 'Rainbow Ward') threatened with mental and physical handicap, his father began writing a journal of poetry which charts not only Ciaran's suffering – his pain and his progress – but also the corresponding inner battle the poet has with his Calvinist beliefs.

Mothachaidh mi ainm an telebhisein
– FIDELITY.
An e facal a tha siud bho Dhia dhomh?
A dhìlseachd riumsa 's mo dhìlseachd Ris?

No a bheil mi gam mhealladh fhìn
's a bheil anns an fhacal seo,
sa bhrù-dhearg seo, sa cheòl seo,
san tinneas seo
ach nithean tubaisteach gun chiall?
I notice the name of the television
– FIDELITY
Is that a word from God to me?
His faithfulness to me and mine to Him?
Or am I kidding myself,
and the truth is that this word,
this robin, this music,
this illness
are all meaningless accidents?

There are other voices here. *The Wizard of Oz*, for example, is quoted at length and alluded to frequently. This enriches the book and gives it a welcome, magical dimension – not to mention the quiet thrill one gets from reading excerpts of *The Wizard of Oz* in Gaelic. (English versions are also supplied!)

MacFhionnlaigh does not always translate exact literal versions of the Gaelic. It is almost though certain poems ('Neamhnaid'/ *'Pearl'* is a good example) have separate lives in the different versions. They are sisters rather than twins. In one sense, this means that a Gaelic reader gets a little more out of it than a non-Gaelic speaker would. But, often, providing good English language translations of Gaelic originals necessitates creative thinking and no writer should be expected to apologise for that. The book implements some novel gaelicisations of 'modern' words (eg 'steatasgop' for 'stethoscope', 'sgitsifrineach' for 'schizophrenic', 'iogart' for 'yoghurt' etc). MacFhionnlaigh is not afraid to push language. In his preface poem, he states:

I am a cryogenic genie –
bottled
on the pelagic floor.
A jurassic insect.

Not the kind of thing found in Gaelic poetry everyday. MacFhionnlaigh is also good at evoking real emotions through simple language. Here he describes a heavy-footed doctor running past:

A' ruith! A' ruith! A' sior ruith!
Na choineanach geal a' ruith seachad orm sìos
tunail.

Fadalach! Fadalach! Ro fhadalach!
Agus mise nam Ailis 's mi cho beag
's cho bàn ri luchag.
Running! Running! Forever running!
He, the White Rabbit,
running past me down the tunnel.
Late! Late! Too late!
And me, Alice, small and pale
as a mouse.

In 'Aisling Eile'/ '*Another Dream*' MacF-
hionnlaigh uses the simple image of a lift ris-
ing to symbolise the helpless distance he feels
between himself and his son "a' sìor fhàs nas
lugha"/ "*growing smaller and smaller*". A
number of poems are successful and haunting
because they are simple and so speak directly:

'S e pileachan buidhe a bh' anns a t-
'Sinemet'.
B' iad seo 'clachan-creadha' beaga
ar Rathaid Bhreigich Bhuidhe.

The Sinemet tablets are yellow.
These were to be the minute bricks
which paved our Yellow Brick Road.

Some poems are less successful. One –
about a playleader named Dorothy – ends:

Agus 's ann an dràsta fhèin a tha mi a'toirt
fa-near cho freagarrach 's a bha ainm Dorothy
dham phlana-sa.

And it is only now that I have noticed
just how suitable was Dorothy's name
to my master plan!

This seems an unusually weak ending for a
poet of MacFhionnlaigh's calibre. Compare
that with the startling conclusion to the poem
'Na Dineasaran'/ '*The Dinosaurs*':

Bha an Triceratops boireann a bha seo 's a h-
àl ann.
Sheas sinn aig an rèile le càch a chum sùil a
thoirt oirre.
'S e an rud a dhrùidh orm, ge-ta,
gun do mhothaich mi nach b' ann air an din-
easar
idir a bha dlùth-aire feadhainn
ach air Ciaran.

There was this female Triceratops with her
young.
We stood with others at the rail to look at it.
What affected me, though, was to notice how
many folk
were not looking at the dinosaur
but at Ciaran.

Bogha-frois san Oidhche is a valuable work
by one of today's best Gaelic's poets. It is also
a brave and honest journal by an anguished,
loving father. Either way, it is unforgettable.

Ainmeil an Eachdraidh, edited by Ruar-
aidh MacThomais, is a collection of 12
essays by 9 writers about people 'famous in
history', most of whom had a connection
with Scotland. It is rare to find a book in
which Julius Caesar nestles beside James
Watt, Alexander Carmichael beside Jock
Stein. While such an anthology is to be
lauded in principle, I was irritated that only
two women, (Mairi Mhòr nan Oran and Flora
MacDonald) merit inclusion. Whether this is
because all the contributors are male, such a
basic imbalance should have been addressed
at the contribution-seeking stage. Co-dhiù,
among the men included are entrepreneurs,
agitators, inventors and writers. The book
contains black and white photographs which
mostly add to one's appreciation of the char-
acters described. (I particularly liked those of
Jock Stein, face a-grin and glowing with
pride, and Julius Caesar's statue, frozen in
magisterial ambition.)

This book is full of interesting facts. I
didn't know that James Watt married his
cousin, that Iain MacMhuirich frequented
both Protestant and Catholic churches. And
what about poor Fionnghala NicDhòmhnaill
(Flora MacDonald):

. . . a bharrachd air na thachair ann an 1746
agus ann an Ameireaga (far an do chaill i
mòran de rudan prìseil, agus far an do
rinneadh mòran geur-leanmhainn oirre
fhèin agus air Gàidheil eile airson a bhith air
taobh na Riaghaltais an Cogadh na Saorsa),
thuit i air a'bhàta nuair a bha i a'tilleadh a
Alba Nuaidh agus chaidh a goirteachadh is
bhrist i a gàirdean; theabadh a bàthadh an
dèidh Dùn Eideann fhàgail ann an 1748;
chaill i dithis mhac; agus bha gainne airgid
oirre fhèin is air Ailean cuid mhath dhem
beatha. Bha i glè bhreòite mun do chaochail
i, is cha d'fhuair i idir saoghal fada.

A side to NicDhòmhnaill's life is encapsu-
lated here which not everybody knows about.
Although this is a fairly sober, fact-heavy

book, it nonetheless has a quirky resonance by virtue of the unpredictable nature of history. Trivia fans as well as scholars will enjoy this book. (When Michael Faraday first demonstrated how bringing a wire near a magnet generates some electricity, the experts at the conference regarded this as little more than a child's toy.) I could go on!

All these essays are interesting and some, such as Dòmhnall Eairdsidh Dòmhnallach's overview of Alasdair MacGilleMhìcheil's life and work, are beautifully written. In many respects this book would be useful in an academic context – not just for students of Gaelic language but of general historical and cultural studies but I would also highly recommend it to anyone with an interest in people!

Chì Mi: Bàrdachd Dhòmhnaill Iain Dhonnchaidh/ I See: The Gaelic Poetry of Donald John MacDonald might seem pricey at £12.99 paperback, but Birlinn are to be congratulated on such an elegant collection. This is the first comprehensive book of the South Uist bard's work to be published. It contains an introduction, notes, photographs, and parallel translations of 108 poems or hymns. Bill Innes has done a sterling job. His introduction, covering a biography of the poet, an examination of his poetry in context, and a word on the translations, exemplary. The translations themselves are quite superb, too.

It is Bill Innes himself who correctly points out the book's critical flaw:

> The bard's output ranged from doggerel to the metaphysical. By including the former and some of the run-of-the-mill early poems there is a risk of devaluing the truly great.

I cannot disagree with that.

> However, the humorous songs bear witness to a vanished way of life, and it is hoped that this astonishingly versatile range of material may hold something for everyone.

I'm not convinced that overall quality should be sacrificed for versatility. This collection would have been stronger if it were shorter than its 369 pages. Sometimes more is less.

MacDonald's father was a seanchaidh, or traditional storyteller, and his uncle was the celebrated poet Domhnall Ruadh Phaislig. As was common at the time, MacDonald left school at 14 to work on the croft. He worked, also, on his appreciation of poetry and even as a teenager he mastered the complex metres of the 17th and 18th century bardachd. His youthful excitement at the outbreak of the Second World War did not last long. He spent time as a prisoner of war in Germany. "I learned more in those five years than I could have in 80 years of ordinary living", the bard was to say. His account of this period is published as *Fo Sgàil a 'Swastika*.

The poems appear in some semblance of chronological order and are, as mentioned, of varying quality. Although brought up in a traditional Gaelic milieu, the poetry is far from insular. Indeed, MacDonald's translation of Gray's 'Elegy Written in a Country Churchyard'/ *'Marbhrann Sgrìobhte ann an Cladh san Dùthaich'* is worth the cover price alone. It demonstrates well MacDonald's technical proficiency, preserving the original rhythm and augmenting it with melodious assonance. A number of diverse themes are covered: love, war, Scottish nationalism, abortion (MacDonald was a Catholic and speaks out on behalf of the unborn child in 'An Guth a Broinn na Mathar'/ *'Voice from the Womb'*).

It is interesting that the bard was affected by comments that his Gaelic was so rich that he was running the risk of alienating his audience – even on his native island. The hymns (composed in later life) are written in a relatively simple style and, as Innes points out, "Significantly, they are nowadays the best known of his works".

Some of the poetry in *Chi Mi* is as good as any Gaelic poetry produced this century. In a brilliant, passionate poem entitled simply 'Thusa'/ *'You'*, MacDonald is at his best:

> Gealltanas mar nach do bhruadar
> mi nad shealltainn: seadh, b'e 'n uair seo
> thàinig miann air eòlas caidreach
> na mo smuaintean.
>
> Coileanadh beath' agus nàdair
> coileanadh an àird an lànachd:
> lùghdaich crìochan mòr an t-saoghail
> gu aon àirigh.

*Promise as I dare not dream of
in your eyes: yes, it was then
desire to know your love
entered my thoughts
Fulfilling life and nature
fulfilling them completely:
wide boundaries of the world shrunk
to one shieling.*

On balance this is a hugely enjoyable (if over-generous) book. Innes has done a magnificent job and this book will ensure the poet's reputation lasts as long as people have an interest in Scottish literature.

Kevin MacNeil

Back to the Future

Stolen Light: Selected Poems, Stewart Conn, Bloodaxe, £9.95; *When it Work it Feels Like Play,* Tessa Ransford, Ramsay Head Press, £7.95; *Poems for Bonnie and Josie (I),* Thom Nairn, Dionysia Press, £5.50.

As the new millennium begins, it is perhaps inevitable that artists look backward in the search to define our times. In a superficial sense, the late 20th century art world's shift of scope from the clinically futuristic to the more organic – and more comfortable – recent past, is a predictable security blanket in the face of the unknown. Yet what continues to surprise me is how often this retrospective mood manages to escape nostalgia, instead producing intelligent and sensitive frames through which to view our present. Poetry lends itself particularly well to this role, providing a microcosm in which to observe and interpret a subject, and these three collections are all good examples of this.

Stewart Conn is a well-known name on the literary scene, and much of the work in *Stolen Light* will be familiar to those who have followed his career. Though it does incorporate some new poems, its value as a medium by which to define both human and specifically Scottish identity at the end of this century is more a function of its structure as a whole. It is no new concept to arrange an anthology chronologically; however, the poems within are skilfully chosen so that each section as a unit describes a step in the progression of human experience. The first section is concerned with childhood and the poems are notably lacking in introspection. They show little self-awareness, but a vigilant consciousness of the natural world, underlined by a strong empathy for animals and those who live closest to them ('Simple Light'):

> ... Against the skyline
> nine Shetland ponies
> stand like cut-outs
> fraying tangerine sun.

Yet even in these least-egocentric of poems discord between an explicable past and ambiguous future is evident. There are multiple references to a beloved farm, both in its prosperous heyday and its present state of disintegration, coinciding with the recurrent figure of Todd, the aging horseman. These extremes are highlighted not in so many words, but in the repeated contrast of the organic past and the inorganic present as in 'Todd: a sequence':

> In his mind's eye, the whole yard is teeming
> with horses ...
> the gates behind them clanging ...
>
> The men have started to strip an old van ...
> The dead metal does not ring at all.

Conn's preoccupation with the contrast between past and present solidifies in the middle sections. Human relationships replace the animals of early sections, and subsequently, the ingenuous narrative voice bows to one of great self-awareness, as in 'North Uist':

> Proud of the buffeting
> I'm taking, I feel I belong:
> till I meet a chained mongrel,
> yap-yapping; and an old woman
> who slurches past, head down.

In these sections human relationships and the natural world interrelate as metaphor, and the narrator's disgust with the mechanized present encroaching on the natural past is quite clear. Yet in poems such as 'A Sense of Order' and 'Portents', there is also a compelling forgiveness for the human society which has created this conflict.

Later sections see more humour, as in

'Bedtime Stories', 'In Monte Mario' and the tongue-in-cheek 'Case Histories', with its not-so-subtle criticism of modern psychology. Also later, Conn's characteristic lyricism and fascination with the distant past come into their own. 'Relic', the last of the poem-sequence 'October Week' which ends the fifth section, sets these wheels in motion:

> The elk-skull in the adjoining room
> remains untouched by my presence.
>
> . . . sustaining not merely visions
> of pursuit over rough terrain . . .
>
> but the tremor of millennia
> in the span of those antlers . . .

This sensitivity to the possibility of the co-habitation of past, present – and, inherently, future – comes to greatest fruition in the two elegies of the last section, 'The Ocean of Time', written for George Mackay Brown, and 'Letters to Iain', for Iain Crichton Smith. Together these poems cycles come close to filling the only gap in Conn's repertoire, the 'big' poem. Conn's inherent gentleness in approaching his subjects combine, here, with his deep feeling for two fellow craftsmen, to create truly moving poetry, and a fitting finale to this comprehensive anthology:

> . . . your presence
> all-pervasive:
>
> . . . scratch of pen, salt
> at the pane; word-geese
> massed on the skyline . . .

Tessa Ransford's new book, *When it Works it Feels Like Play,* is another literal look at the conflict between past and present, and its significance for the future. Like Conn, she is as comfortable looking to a general human past for material as she is drawing on her own past. The book has five sections titled: 'Meditative', 'Contemplative', 'Discursive', 'Interpretive' and 'Relative'. Though the content of the poems in each section takes the titles as rough guidelines, the distinctions among them – as among the meanings of the titles themselves – often seem too slight to merit such clearly delineated categorisation.

Perhaps as a result of this emphasis on classification, the collection reads unevenly at times. The poems reflecting on specifics are generally strong, as in 'Kingfisher':

> . . . bluer than sky
> skyer than air
> more air than water
> more water than leaf
> more leaf than light . . .

Those on broader or more ambiguous topics are either flat by comparison or inextricably cerebral, as in the four 'Conception' poems from the section entitled 'Contemplative':

> Conjugation of verbs, to be, to bide, *ich bin,*
> to make a bield on earth, to conjoin
> forces for good, safety, communion.
> I build therefore I am . . .

Having said that, Ransford's is on the whole a straightforward, accessible book, in many ways pleasingly tactile. Like Conn's references to 19th century painters, Ransford's to earlier poets and poems place her work firmly within the European literary tradition, and serve as valuable reference points in looking at human past, present and future.

Where Conn's retrospection is at its best often metaphysical, Ransford's has a direct, personal quality, which allows the poems to move the reader while remaining tangible, as in her tribute to the women left husbandless by the World Wars ('Maiden Aunts') ". . . virginity a kind of hell,/ despised, denied, rejected./ hypocritically respected. . ."

The poem cycle 'In Praise of Libraries', despite its stodgy title, is one of the best of the collection, both for its poetic integrity and its comment on time's ravages of precious bits of humanity. Ransford summarises this idea poignantly in the first section of the cycle:

> We know the causes of death,
> We study and research them.
>
> Of life we know nothing and
> Great libraries have been burnt . . .

'The Book Rediscovered in the Future' is both a nod to this idea, and a clever reiteration of the modern anxiety about what the space age will cost us:

> . . . 'Imagine being able to hold
> in your hand what you read,
> to carry it with you and wear it out
> with your life . . .'

If Ransford's collection doesn't match the lyricism of Conn's, it is nonetheless an intelligent commentary on our present era.

Tom Nairn's collection, *Poems for Bonnie and Josie (I),* is not simple to define. The title is a reference to the Wallace Stevens poem 'Life is Motion'; but beyond this, the collection is lacking the anchors of the past or the anxieties for the future, which are so evident in Conn's and Ransford's work. Instead, the poems wallow in a present which the narrator can no more connect with than he can jettison. His view of the present is at once so bleak and so stagnant, that the title's reference to a joyous and kinetic poem is a bit of a mystery.

The poems are cohesive in that their tone uniformly distances itself from emotion. This works well in the pieces which are focused on something small and specific, as in 'Transience' or the cinematic 'Two Shadows':

Smooth as a crow carrying
Night on his back

The rain comes down over low hills
Still caught up in the sun.

However, in poems such as 'No Random Violence', the formula of detached observation fails to serve the broader and more cerebral subject matter, leaving it incapable of supporting its own weight:

This is here and not here,
life at needle point,
consisting of decisions on
where the needle point ends,
where sharpness and rigidity
give way to infinity.

There is a uniform darkness to the content and a pervasive pessimism in the narrative voice. The book is fraught with death, blood and violence, rendering its few tentative excursions into the realm of emotion – albeit unintentionally – leaden, as in 'Commandos':

And you as close on me
As barnacles, land on me like
A Harrier at dawn: clandestine
Raid on a half-consciousness.

The one, intriguingly warm strain in an otherwise chilly collection consists of a few poems concerned with a female 'you', who remains unnamed. The poems 'When You're Not Here', 'Implicit', 'Taking Steps' and 'Closing on Histories' all infuse a dim colour into the black-and-grey of the rest of the collection. Yet even this strain doesn't end happily:

You've lost your dark power,
I've lost mine,
In each other's eyes
We're too translucent,
These are things we know
But can't quite spell. ('Closing on Histories')

Poems for Bonnie and Josie (I) is perhaps best described as a troubling collection. It affords little comfort, with no means of securing oneself in space and time nor the solid walls of a definable past and imaginable future. Yet perhaps, ultimately, it is the most valuable for what appears to be lacking: it is an undeniably honest assessment of one man's present, despite his clear discomfort with it. It's one worth thinking about.

Sarah Bryant

Raw Talent

Strange Fish; Magi Gibson and Helen Lamb; Duende Press, £5.99: *Leaving You and Leaving You*; Sophie Hannah; *Air for Sleeping Fish*; Gillian Ferguson; *Canuting the Waves*; Jackie Hardy; (all Bloodaxe, £6.95).

Poetry is becoming trendier at the moment. Young, independent publishers are launching funky, new volumes of excellent up-to-the-minute writers and the selection for this particular review is no exception.

Magi Gibson and Helen Lamb have published a terrific collection of poetry called *Strange Fish*, which has a slight gothic touch to it. The characters portrayed are psychologically at the brink with a dark, bitter side to their nature. This gives the book a slightly dynamic, edgy feel. The poems also explore power relations between men and women. The women here are powerful but with unfulfilled desires. These works are offset by atmospheric, pagan-looking illustrations.

Gibson's poems have a predatory theme: 'in the dark of the forest' she writes "you can not shake me off/ I will not let you go". 'Saboteur to Hunter' is quite eerie and original, offering the perspective of the hunted animal:

> I don't want to see
> your human face
> just like you don't want to see
> the soft eye of the doe
> as she twitches on the heather
> life spurting from her breast.

'The Sauce' also examines the animal rights cause. The line "you finally taste the animal in yourself" may make meat-eaters stop and think for its exploration of an alternative viewpoint. Another grim outlook comes from 'The Widow'. One may expect grief at the death of a loved one. Instead the reader is told "with his death/ I seemed to come alive". The death signifies the rejuvenation of the self.

'OnceUponADream' explores the myth of the handsome Prince contrasted with the reality of the slobbering drunk and Helen Lamb's poem, ironically titled 'Married Bliss', similarly writes of lonely relationships that do not fulfil expectations. Family relations are also viewed as awkward. Innocence is bitterly corrupted at childhood, like an Emily Dickinson poem. 'How to Walk in the Dark' and 'The Quiet Daughter', are insightful, communicative poems that use skilful imagery.

> from time to time she'd drag me out
> wear me, dangled prettily
> on the end of her arm –
> the ultimate accessory
> a quiet daughter

But it is not all doom and gloom. These women know how to write tender, skilful love poems that don't sound tacky. 'Guitar' by Gibson stands out. She writes "touch the smooth brown of my body/ till even my hair sings/ with the beauty of it". These sensuous last lines are original, if simply written.

As a collection, I can't recommend it highly enough. Magi Gibson and Helen Lamb are excellent compliments of each other. The poetry is superb, dramatic reading and is accompanied by beautiful illustrations that divide it into natural sections.

Sophie Hannah is similarly a lovely writer. At 28, she has written an accomplished volume of poetry, enough to cause pangs of jealousy in any aspiring writer. Many poems in *Leaving You and Leaving You* are about relationships, occasionally with a fairy-tale/ folk element. 'The Bridging Line' and 'Your Darlings' stand on their own without too much mythical reference, which requires a particularly adept skill.

Her relationship poems are touching with good use of word power: the title poem and 'This Morning in a Black Jag' have real poignancy and honesty. Many of her poems involve travelling, leaving relationships and moving jobs which gives a sense of unsettledness, particularly 'Never Away', 'Driving Me Away' and 'Leaving You and Leaving You'. Occasionally the poems are absurd with a quirky humour, for example 'If People Disapprove of You' and 'Men to Burn':

> The same men every year
> though we have men to burn
> we have sealed off that idea.
> It is still one man's turn.

She ends a brutal poem with tender lines "A good man in the first place/ makes for better effigies". At times her poems get a little obscure and self-referential – a natural downside to writing with such intense emotions. On the whole, this is a fine book of poetry.

Gillian Ferguson is probably better known than Sophie Hannah for writing in *The Scotsman*. Her work in *Air for Sleeping Fish* is abstract and presented as a series of sharp images, not necessarily connected with each other. Her poems also tend to personify nature: like a dozen haikus weaving into one another. It is an interesting form, concise and vivid, although I felt occasional elaboration was needed, for example in 'In Hospital-Land'. In the more emotional poems her voice is slightly too controlled.

Some of her work is about the writing process. 'Opium Poet' has fetching lines, "Open to the world/ beneath the veil of stone, soil, skin". She has also tackled difficult themes admirably, for example 'War in the Gulf'. Her lines have an effective sting.

> There is no right
> or wrong anymore –

only people
plumbed with blood
cocooned in whole skins,
fearing sleep
in treeless lands.

Canuting the Waves by Jackie Hardy has a similar style, working with striking images, predominately of marine life. Although most Scottish nature poems have a habit of being contrived, Hardy has a natural humour and clever manipulation of words. 'Wet Feet' and 'Cetacean' are worth looking at. One phrase from 'Cetacean' "sounding in her monstrous body/ vibrating through her massive bones" reads beautifully. The image of the selkie is prevalent here, a figure which often captures the imagination in poetry. Like Gillian Ferguson she works with distinct images that look like a group of haikus threaded together.

A more technological poem 'Computer Aided Design' has a modern slant on the Creation: "God scrolled through His works, monitored progress./ God saw that it was good and that His name was in the hi-scores". 'The Essential Guide to Astral Travel' is another hilarious piece, an amusing take on the practicalities of space travel. 'insects' is also funny, but more focused on word play: "two flies settle/ on a romance".

Her poems lack the attitude and excited imagination of Magi Gibson's work and occasionally become loose and self-referential, for example in 'Dora Takes the Stand'. However, the book has its fair share of gems and if you enjoy a sassy humour and colourful images this may be worth browsing.

What strikes me about these collections is their diversity of approach. Each volume switches effortlessly through time periods of past, present and future. They confront varied issues from relationships to nationality to moral ethics to the work place, so that most people can find something of interest. Their diverse themes make them more accessible, and they do not lack individuality, as the experimentation of style in each provides the edge that is often required for poetry to work.

Marie Carter

The Etruscan Readers

The Etruscan Readers, Etruscan Books, £7.50 each, 9 vols., £50.00 set.

I, Helen MacDonald, Gael Turnbull, Nicholas Johnson
II, Tom Scott, Sorley MacLean, Hamish Henderson
III, Maggie O'Sullivan, David Gascoyne, Barry MacSweeney
IV, Maurice Scully, Bob Cobbing, Carlyle Reedy
V, Tom Raworth, Bill Griffiths, Tom Leonard
VI, Robin Blaser, Barbara Guest, Lee Harwood
VII, Alice Notley, Wendy Mulford, Brian Coffey
VIII, Tina Darragh, Douglas Oliver, Randolph Healy
IX, Meg Bateman, Nicholas Moore, Fred Beake.

In 1997 Etruscan Books, a Devon-based publisher, launched a series of poetry anthologies under the collective title of *The Etruscan Readers*, with Nicholas Johnson as general editor. The series, now complete, comprises nine books, any of which would be a valuable addition to the library of anyone interested in the development of 20th century poetry.

The format is the same for each book: a substantial collection of work by three different poets, some of them well-known, some of them new voices, offering an eclectic mix of traditional forms and newer experimental work. Of the 27 poets included in the series, 7 are Scottish, the others English, Irish, American, and Canadian. Women poets are well represented and it is noticeable that some of the most innovative work is by women.

Most of the work is unavailable elsewhere, as it is the stated intention of the series to restore to permanent print work which is no longer retained in publication, or which has been previously uncollected in book form. Each of these volumes would merit an exclusive review, but here it is only possible to give a flavour of the series as a whole.

There are many unexpected treasures in these collections. For example, *Reader I* contains Gael Turnbull's previously uncollected and disturbing poem 'The Ballad of Rillington Place' about a tragic miscarriage of justice. *Reader III* includes a number of recently rediscovered poems by David Gascoyne from 1936-7; the same volume also sees the first publication of Barry McSweeney's heart-breaking 'Finnbar's Lament' (which was due to be anthologised in 1993 but the entire edition was mysteriously destroyed following a take-over by Rupert Murdoch): ". . . Her cloakclasp shining in starlight at the edge of an ocean/ Her plaid flapping in the southern wind at the world's rim".

Limiting the number of poets to three per volume allows for the inclusion of longer poems. It also means that individual poets are given the space and freedom to represent the variety within their own work. For instance, the work by Gael Turnbull in *Reader I* spans several decades and demonstrates wide range from haunting lyric to satirical verse. Through many poems runs a thread of social concern and the struggle for individual integrity, as in the American poet Alice Notley's questioning interior dialogues as she strives to make sense of the human condition through dreams and memories (*Reader VII*): "don't we possess, abuse it/ together, this country from which we abuse/ the substance of the world?"

Randolph Healy's extraordinary poem 'Arbor Vitae' in *Reader VIII* is an impassioned plea for deaf children to be allowed to use sign language, and Healy draws a parallel between the suppression of its use by educators and the attempts by the English to obliterate the use of the Irish language in the past:

Central doctrines:
That true language is lingual;
that one form of expression excludes another;
that failure is due to lack of effort.

Noticeable throughout is the cross-cultural nature of the subject matter which often crosses boundaries of nationality and time. Thus Douglas Oliver writes of the problems of ethnic diversity in Paris (*Reader VIII*), Nicholas Johnson mourns the death of the wandering American singer/songwriter Townes Van Zandt (*Reader I*) and Wendy Mulford (*Reader VII*) slips into the footsteps of St Francis and St Clare, or the 13th century Rule for Anchoresses:

. . . have your hair cut
four times a year to disburden your head

. . . ye shall not possess any beast
except only a cat.

Emphasising this cultural cross-fertilization there are a number of translations, including Brian Coffey's sequence inspired by Aragon, Eluard, Verlaine and others (*Reader VII*), Hamish Henderson's previously uncollected translations from Cavafy and Montale, and Tom Scott's translations of Baudelaire and Dante (*Reader II*). *Reader IX* includes Gaelic/English poems by Meg Bateman.

Reader II (entitled *Pervigilium Scotiae* – 'Scotland's Vigil') is Johnson's homage to a generation of Scottish poets in the *makar* tradition. It has a bi-lingual gathering of influential early work by Sorley MacLean including poems from *Dàin do Eimhir*, and three poems which were the last he ever wrote. It also contains a sequence by Hamish Henderson written during the early days of the Second World War, *The Flyting o' Life and Daith*, and the words and music of some of his best-loved songs. Also included is some of Tom Scott's most scathing polemical satire.

Another feature is diversity of technique. Experimental poets such as Maggie O'Sullivan, Tina Darragh and Nicholas Johnson explore the aural and visual possibilities of sound and text, where often the exact position of a word on the page is significant, and where the syntax can be a challenge to the reader who has to work hard to extract the meaning.

Alongside this is the variety of styles to be found within each volume, as where the vibrant imagery of Tom Raworth's 'Lions in the Corner' rubs shoulders with Tom Leonard's dialect sequence 'Hesitations' in *Reader V*, or the classicism of Brian Coffey contrasts sharply with Alice Notley's dream fragments in *Reader VII*. Similarly, Readers IV and VI between them cover a wide spectrum: the Trans-atlantic world view of Robin Blaser; Irish lyric; London concrete; Lee Harwood's fragmented collages of love and loss.

Altogether this is a fascinating and unusual series which takes the reader along some main highways and also off the beaten track. Singly or collectively they would make an interesting addition to any poetry shelf.

The books, which are well produced in

strong paperback may be ordered from Peter Riley Books, 27 Sturton Street, Cambridge, CB1 2QG. (£7.50 + £1.00 p&p)

Heather Scott

Catalogue

As an American seeing my fellow citizens have their pictures taken next to the Mel Gibson statue at the foot of the Wallace monument, it is refreshing to come across a detailed and accurate account of Scotland's Wars of Independence. Peter Traquair's *Freedom's Sword* (HarperCollins, £16.99) is the perfect alternative for anybody whose Scottish history comes from *Braveheart*, though it is extensive enough to require a vested interest from the reader. It makes a fair attempt at presenting an objective representation of the events, and though it does include its share of speculation, it doesn't claim to be anything more than just that. Its intention is quite clearly stated in the introduction as "neither a Scottish history of the wars, nor is it an English apology: this is a history of an island at war". This is a fair statement, as the author was educated in both Scotland and England, though at times an undertone of defensiveness could be drawn from theories of motivations for English actions. This is not to suggest bias, merely a responsiveness to inaccuracies to which Traquair may suspect the reader has been exposed. The style is quite comprehensive and relatively engaging, and not be lost in specialised jargon.

Also of historical interest is John S Gibson's *The Gentle Lochiel* (NMS Publishing, £5.99) which focuses on Donald Cameron of Lochiel, described by Sir Walter Scott as "the most amiable and accomplished of the Highland heroes". A little more in-depth for those already familiar with Jacobite history and the events of 1745, this book presents wider sources of information than were known previously, including accounts by Lochiel himself. Gibson proves himself to be a competent and skilful storyteller here.

A treat for admirers of Sir Walter Scott is *The Voyage of the Pharos* (Scottish Library Association, £7.50), his diary detailing an adventurous six-week sailing trip round Scotland in 1814 with the Commissioners of the Northern Lights, inspecting lighthouses and new lighthouse sites. Scott relates stories of encounters with people in the Highlands and islands when much was changing in history, using all his charm and vivid poetic detail. He describes the experience as an extremely enjoyable trip, and his enthusiasm for what he sees and experiences is contagious.

Outside the Scottish arena comes *The Key to Our Aborted Dreams* translated by Anne-Marie Glasheen (Peter Lang), an anthology of five plays by contemporary Belgian women dealing with women's frustration at trying to achieve their ambitions. *Claire Lacombe* by Michèle Fabien offers more in feminist philosophy than a good dramatic piece, though it does contain interesting perspectives in its exploration of a woman's role post-French Revolution and the lack of improvement in her situation. Ironic comment on 'strength' and who is expected to have it in a husband-wife relationship is made:

> Can you let him see you cry, tired, depressed, hurt, miserable, like him? No! You don't have the right to be like him! You have to be different, the last thing he wants is to see himself when he looks at you.

Alma Mahler by Françoise Lalande is not so much a play as a poem meant for performance, an unrhymed ballad even, telling an unrhymed story of a woman leading an unrhymed life. In her constant dissatisfaction with love, relationships and self-identity, any woman would feel some resonance with this character. Also included are works by Pascale Tison, Liliane Wouters, Françoise Lison-Leroy and Colette Nys-Mazure. There is a running theme of women being compromised and making great sacrifices for love, whatever the cultural, political or historical setting. As with much translation, the quality of language and style in this collection is unavoidably compromised, but for the one who loves to analyse, however, these plays offer quite a bit of substance to ponder.

A woman who has certainly not let herself be compromised, Rigoberta Menchù, Guatemalan Indian leader and Nobel Peace Prize winner, has produced the second instalment of her autobiography, *Crossing Borders* (Verso, £17), following *I, Rigoberta Menchù*. *Crossing Borders* discusses her return from twelve years in exile and her winning of the prize. She writes of what her home, family and community mean to her, relating the horrible truths of injustice, violence and racism with spirit, hope and strength. Her account is eye-opening, moving, disturbing and yet warmly written, taking politics back to the personal level where they are proved inseparable. What is truly inspiring is the extent to which she listens to her heart and her dreams, staying determined, clear-headed and uncompromised out of deep affection and love for her people, their way of life and environment.

Useful to all aspiring playwrights is the aptly titled *How to Write a Play* by David Carter ('Teach Yourself Books, £6.99), full of sound advice and structural tips for both getting started and following through on your next, well, dramatic masterpiece, or rather a typically well-crafted yet unexceptional play –about as far as this book could take you on its own. You'll either find it quite useful for overcoming a slump of writer's block or be intimidated by all its categories and steps which may cloud your creative process, in which case perhaps set it aside at first and use its advice for editing a second draft. Carter recognises this need for flexibility in the use of his guidance and even recommends you don't follow it exactly. Other types of writers could also find it useful for bringing more drama and life into their story-spinning, but as with most books on writing, take it for what it's worth and then go your own way.

For some real-life drama, try reading *The Guest From the Future* by György Dalos (John Murray, £17.99) which details the encounter between Isaiah Berlin and poet Anna Akhmatova in Leningrad in 1945, an almost chance meeting which was to transform Russian literary history. It is a love story leading to tragedy and persecution for Akhmatova, and to some of her greatest love poetry. Told from Akhmatova's viewpoint, Dalos collected information from interviews with Sir Isaiah Berlin and others who knew Akhmatova, compiling this into a well-told and heart-felt account of all that transpired.

A far greater literary work (though not always so acclaimed) expressing thoughts on Scotland's history through fiction is James Hogg's *Queen Hynde*, the sixth volume in a running collection of works by James Hogg published by Edinburgh University Press (eds Suzanne Gilbert and Douglas S Mack, £35). *Queen Hynde*, from 1824, is an ambitious epic about the beginnings of the Scottish nation told with the clever wit, mastery of lyric and subversive undertone characteristic to Hogg, the uneducated shepherd and unlikely candidate for immortal literary fame. Clearly presented, this edition does him justice as a great literary figure with an in-depth introduction detailing his peculiar situation and society's reaction to it. *The Collected Works* will continue to republish many of Hogg's works which are out of print.

John Donald brings us *The Historic Houses of Edinburgh* by Joan M Wallace (£10.95), a updated and revised second edition. This illustrated guide to historic houses from the old town to the new town to the greater Edinburgh area provides an index of people as well as houses and many interesting titbits on the evolution of life in Edinburgh as seen by its architecture. Though not entirely complete, it contains a good survey of buildings from different periods and comments on how they have been adapted to present-day use. The short descriptions are informative, but to get the most out of this book one would have to visit the houses themselves. Ideal for either the Edinburgh resident curious about the intriguing old house on the corner or for the visitor wanting an educational, self-led tour.

If you think you might be interested in Catalan literature, *Catalan Literature: A General View* (Generalitat de Catalunya, Department de Cultura, Institució de les Lletres Catalanes, Portal de Santa Madrona 6-8, 08001 Barcelona) provides a brief and unintimidating introduction, bringing Catalan literature into the foreign eye, confident of its worthiness to be known. Its three essays by Isidor Cònsul, Vincenç Llorca and Àlex Broch take you on an easy journey from medieval to contemporary literature of all types. A good read though at times its brevity is excessive, leading occasionally to meaningless lists of authors.

From Scottish Studies International comes a study by Cornelia Jumpertz-Schwab, *The Development of the Scots Lexicon and Syntax in the 16th Century under the Influence of Translations from Latin* (Peter Lang) which is, exactly as its lengthy title suggests, a demonstration of how Latin has influenced Scots which, in the 15th and 16th centuries, was of no doubt a language on its own, its status only later reduced to a variation of English. *The Low Countries: Arts and Society in Flanders and the Netherlands* (Flemish-Netherlands Foundation 'Stichting Ons Erfdeel', Murissonstraat 260, 8930 Rekkem, Flanders, Belgium, £40) is a yearbook for 1998-99 with all sorts of excerpts from Dutch-speaking cultures for the English-speaking world. Extensive and complete with colour photos, though not so flash as to live up to its price.

And finally, for anyone interested in further exploring Scottish literary heritage is the handy *Waterstone's Guide to Scottish Books* edited by Neil Johnstone (Waterstone's, £3.99) which gives brief descriptions of a wide selection of titles from every time period and genre. It is well-organised alphabetically and by category and features articles by established authors recommending their favourites, such as Janice Galloway's account of her liking for the works of Alasdair Gray. It provides a helpful reference for those looking for quality books to read, and is useful to those simply seeking to gain an overall grasp on Scottish literature and its authors.

Maryann Ullmann

Pamphleteer

Of the poetry reviewed here the book from Enitharmon is most promising. Though elegantly produced and including a wide range of poems, their standard is variable. Most interesting are Jeremy Hooker's *Our Lady of Europe* (£8.95) and Kevin Crossley-Holland's *Poems from East-Anglia* (£7.95). Hooker, writing about barbarity, is at his best when he confronts his sense of horror in 'Remembering Berlin'. In the first section, however, 'Troy of the North' his observations are prone to dead-endedness, the poems often understated and baldly descriptive. It may have to do with his perception of the North; a landscape where the sea effaces any act of construction, "After long labour the place/ is a patchwork of water and earth". And the poems too are a landscape where it would be naive to build up images. Kevin Crossley-Holland's attitude contrasts with Hooker's. He acknowledges the sea's rapacity but considers the "no-man's land" of the marsh to be a site of richness. The sinister landscape

> screaming poppies
> a gull perched on a salt-crusted ploughshare
> and a gull, a litter of blood-tarred feathers
> festering

is underlain with the fertilising richness of decomposition and yields "A veil of butterflies, opalescent". Whilst Crossley-Holland finds beauty in a hostile environment he admits in 'The Great Painter' that it is inaccessible: "Who said anything about comfort?/ Those syllables do not rhyme/ With zinc slates or ice-bright sky".

Hilary Davies demonstrates in *In a Valley of this Restless Mind* (£7.95) an extraordinary capacity for breadth and depth of empathy. She imagines remote lives with a convincing level of detail, especially in 'When the Animals Came' where she assumes the voice of a French cave-dweller in the Upper Palaeolithic. However, her writing is more historically interesting than poetic and her extended prosaic forms over-express her environment. In *A Madder Ghost* (£7.95) Martyn Crucefix's best poems are the shorter ones in the

'Ante' and 'Post' sections. Here he writes with integrity about the anticipation and birth of his son, especially 'Pieta', describing the labour, "you sink with your back to me/ slung limp from my arms/ like the impossibility of flight". The central sequence 'Belly Pains on Princelet St' where he attempts to adopt the voice of his Hugenot ancestors and their persecution, and deal with his father's fears and his own infirmity, simply tries to do to much.

Phoebe Hesketh's *A Box of Silver Birch* (£5.95) is prone to awkward self-consciousness: "no wonder poets 'Rage/ rage against the dying of the light'" ('Martyr') though many of her other poems are rooted in sharp observation. Her best writing deals with ageing – 'Retired' and 'The Island' appear side by side and offer the two contrasting views of acceptance and fear. Joe Cushnan's *Emerald Blue* (Poetry Monthly Press, 39 Cavendish Rd, Long Eaton, Nottingham NG10 4HY, £1.20) is similarly self-conscious. He wants us to reconstruct established meanings: the title requires us to reconsider the nature of 'blueness'. But his selection of metaphors is annoyingly random. His work is shadowed by an awareness of poetic persona and the tired old theme of a writer's sense of inadequacy, not about the complexities of the task, but compared with established writers. It's most glaring in 'Postcards from Seamus Heaney' where Cushnan expresses delight in Heaney's comment "Good to hear from you". His apt comment on his own poems "some good, some bad, but at least I'm in there writing".

Caroline Natzler in *Speaking the Wetlands* (Pikestaff Press, Ellon House, Harpford, Sidmouth, Devon EH10 0NH, £3) deals with insecurity successfully in 'A Poet's Education'. She is concerned about which kinds of experience are 'poetic' and proves that poetry really does come from lives where "My home was pretty quiet/ and I read a lot".

Dennis O'Donnell's *Two Clocks Ticking* (Curly Snake Publishing, Unit 1, Abbeymount Techbase, Edinburgh EH8 8EJ, £5.95), likewise, is a brilliantly observed collection. These lines from 'Selections from the Blackburn Summer Catalogue' are reminiscent of MacCaig: "a young blackbird cock . . . turning its head from side to side/ as if it had tried on several beaks/ and liked the yellow one best". O'Donnell's often bizarre metaphors give a sense of surprise accompanied by acceptance that the images used have been the right ones: "a girl is eating a kiwi fruit/ she delicately decapitates the hedgehog's egg/ before spooning out the sweet green yolk".

The pamphlets from Vennel Press (8a Richmond Rd, Staines TW18 2AB) form part of their 'Brief Pleasures' collection and demonstrate the variety of content and quality to be found in poetry pamphlets. A book characterised by its brevity is an ideal vehicle for haiku or similar compact forms, something Gael Turnbull's collection *Amorous Greetings in Terms of . . .* is apparently aware of. The approach is successful in 'In terms of a botanical observation':

> May our love multiply
> unlike the bamboo
> which has never been known
> to flower in cultivation,

but subsequent poems lack the necessary tension and fall out as banal observations – unusual for Turnbull whose work is generally highly original. Duncan McGibbon's offering *Channel* tries an unfortunate alternative approach – to convey his subject by listing with precision the sum of its parts (apparently aided by a *Collins Guide to Sea Life*). He leaps from his "crusty mosaic of sponges" to the "groins of mussels" to "barnacles/ haggard with stealth" without working any one metaphor for possible effect. Finally, Elizabeth James's *World of Interiors* is a peculiar collection. James collects images as if they were artefacts – soullessly. "I believe that every environment can be improved/ and made more beautiful. I like my life". This pamphlet is more reminiscent of literary theory than poetry, but worth reading for the shiver down the spine and clarity of language.

Alfred Milne's *Benchmarks* (Alfred David Editions, 3a Palace Rd, London SW2 3DY, £5) is an inaccessible volume which nevertheless is worth dipping into for its comprehensive overturn of lexicon. It will take an optimistic reader to follow a narrative through this epic, but lovers of thesauri and dictionaries may admire his manipulation of words for meaning and melopoetic effect:

Dextrorse aromas burn
sky high off acid wits
we're not in good odour
you and I, nor fit for the
patience of piecemeal
latinity, dog eat dog or
slow barques (!) to rhodes
you cannot be serious.

No, you can't. Virtuosic use of language with little depth beneath the ornamentation.

If Milne is looking to make us rethink our language-associations, Alan Riach seems to have a similar end in mind albeit using a different approach. In his translation of Dante *The Vision of Hell* (akros, 33 Lady Nairn Ave, Kirkcaldy, Fife, £2.55) Riach uses the journey through the realms of Hell to draw an analogy with the effects of media on our perception of horror. "The devils fight among themselves./ More boiling pitch. More suffering. But it's like watching TV. Who cares any more? How can you?" His comment is an important one – images of the most horrific events easily become meaningless. It is art's (including poetry's) responsibility to sharpen our perceptions. This perhaps validates the reader having to invest hard work here. Riach uses a fragmentary approach similar to Eliot's *The Waste Land*: the onus is on the reader to expand the references: "how like Mahler in D, its steady still weird opening" and "Religion? Just another failed attempt/ to make art popular said Ezra, He's here, somewhere."

Chris North's collection about clearing landmines (*Risky Business*, Cthonia Press, Hansville, 2 Newton Rd, Innellan, Dunoon, Argyll PA23 7TR) highlights the different strains we need to put language under (and the different ways we need to read). Unfortunately it isn't as successful as poetry. But to comment on the inadequacies of North's language here would be to misplace the book's proper relevance with the same kind of blind-

ness that North decries in 'These Things I Keep Inside': "You are to clear the village for the press/ make sure that it's safe for them to film". Brian Scates's *Star Sonnets for Kathleen Curran* (Brian Scates, 134 Bargery Rd, London DE6 2LR) traces the process of mourning. Scates's approach to the sonnet form is traditional and his language is burdened by the syntactic awkwardness of an archaic mode. However, a pleasing feature is the writer's apparent progression through grief, to the final sonnet where Curran goes unmentioned, signals a wider perspective.

Whether intended to shock us into clarity or just shock us (the latter most likely) *My Elvis Blackout* (Crump, Clocktower Press, Breckan, Stennesss, Orkney KW16 3EZ, £4) is a surreal series of 'shorts' that reads like pamphlet *Pulp Fiction*. This quote from 'Elvis, Fat Fucked Up Foetus' is typical:

When he was a foetus, Elvis used to wait till his Mom was asleep, carefully remove his umbilical cord, sneak out of her insides and head off into town ... 'Now's the time to rip stuff off', he figured. 'Before I get any goddamn fingerprints'.

Unlike North and Scates's collections, there is no redeeming quality to this pamphlet.

Finally James McGonigal's *Driven Home* (Mariscat Press, 3 Mariscat Rd, Glasgow G41 4ND, £4.50), is a jump back into a more self-referential mode. These over-imaged poems either overwork metaphors, "some men who could track for days, with arrows dipped/ in deadly irony, and never fetch a single poem home" and or lose control of them. He leaps from the forest image to "the alphabet ocean . . .waves unfolding over like pages of vast foreign dictionaries". It is worth a read for the eponymous poem 'Driven Home' where his imagery is energetic and less self-conscious,

here we are on Purgatory's M8
blinking awake by floodlit Kirk o'Shotts
where rusted tv masts and riding lights
pitch above Central Scotland's forest waves.

This is the value of pamphlets – apart from the variety they offer – the chance for such resonant moments to be made public.

Jenny Hadfield

Notes on Contributors

Gregor Addison was born in 1966. After attending Newbattle Abbey College, he studied Gaelic and English at Aberdeen University, and is now a part-time lecturer at Dumbarton and Clydebank.

Sheena Blackhall has published over 18 books to date including short story collections and poetry mainly in Doric/ North East Scots. An illustrator and singer, she is a member of the Aberdeen Gaelic choir. Her ambition is one day to visit India and Japan.

Sarah Bryant, originally from American, has lived in Edinburgh for over three years. she currently has one novel under consideration in America, and is revising a second.

Susan Castillo: originally from the American South, she lived in Portugal for many years before coming to Scotland and has published poetry and fiction in Britain and the US. she is, for her sins, Head of English Literature at Glasgow University.

Samantha Coleman came to Edinburgh for inspiration. She writes fiction that she hopes is a reflection of today's society and the role that people play within it.

Gerrie Fellows's poetry sequence *The Powerlines*, which explores her New Zealand upbringing, is due from Polygon in Spring 2000. Polygon also published *Technologies and Other Poems.*

Iain Galbraith's recent publications include editions of Conrad's *Nostromo* and Scott's *Old Mortality*, as well as German versions of Edna Walsh's *Disco Pigs* and John King's *The Football Factory.*

George Gunn's recent play *Atomic City* recently toured Scotland under the auspices Scottish Hydro-Electric.

Xanthe Hall was born in Dundee in 1959 and grew up in Scotland and England. In 1985, she left Britain for West Berlin. She is presently working as the Director of a large peace organisation in Germany.

David Hastie is completeing his Ph.D thesis, 'Post-war Scottish Drama' at the University of Aberdeen. He loves teaching, hates admin, lives in a cottage with a sea-view and would love to get his golf handicap sorted out.

Nasim Marie Jafry lives in Edinburgh. Previous work has appeared in *New Writing Scotland*, *NorthWords*, *Writing Women* and *Cutting Teeth*. She was shortlisted for the 1999 RLS Memorial Award.

Ian McDonough: originally from Brora, Sutherland, now working as a mediator in Edinburgh. Currently working on a series of poems on particle physics for Strathclyde University, despite having been ejected from the school science class. SAC award 1999. *A Rising Fever* shortly to be published by Kettalonia.

Angus McFarlane: Born in St Andrews in 1952. Finally escaped teaching English in secondary schools. Now enjoys setting cats among post-modernist pigeons.

Kevin MacNeil was born and raised on the Isle of Lewis. He currently holds the first Iain Crichton Smith Writing Fellowship based in Skye. *Love and Zen in the Outer Hebrides* is available from Canongate Books.

Edwin Morgan's latest books are *Virtual and Other Realities* (Carcanet), *Doctor Faustus* (new version of Marlowe's play, Canongate) and *Demon* (Mariscat). *New Selected Poems* is due from Carcanet in April 2000, and is a Poetry Book Society Special Recommendation.

Donald S Murray if from Lewis, but now lives in Benbecula. A collection of his short stories – *Special Deliverance* – has been published by Scottish Cultural Press.

David Nicol: Born Dundee 1962. Various occupations including forestry. Received SAC writer's bursary 1997. Lately finished (!?) writing a novel. Lives in Aberdeen.

Heather Scott born London 1935. Married poet Tom Scott 1963. Has occasionally contributed poetry and prose to magazines.

Valerie Thornton is a creative writing tutor who lives in Glasgow. She has been publishing poems and short stories for many years and was shortlisted for the Macallan in 1992.

Stanley Trevor: from South Africa now living in the Highlands. Publications include *Collected Poems 1973-1997* and *The Way of the World* (with Pierre Watter). The only white poet invited to read at a memorial reading for Steve Biko and Robert Sobukwe. Have poems will travel.

Billy Watt's poetry pamphlet, *Porpoises on the Moray Firth*, was recently published by Redbeck Press; his short story chapbook, *Ways of Seeing, Ways of Falling*, was put out by Piper's Ash.